Achieving Financial Independence as a Freelance Writer

FACT OF LIFE
(GENERAL)

The more interests you acquire, the more interesting you become.

FACT OF LIFE
(WRITER-SPECIFIC)

The more interests you acquire, the more specialization opportunities exist, the greater the demand for your services.

Achieving Financial Independence as a Freelance Writer

Ray Dreyfack

Blue Heron Publishing § Portland, Oregon

Achieving Financial Independence as a Freelance Writer
By Ray Dreyfack

Copyright © 2000 by Raymond Dreyfack.

All rights reserved. No part of this book may be reproduced or transmitted in any form, by any means, without the written permission of the publisher, except that quotes from the text may be freely used in reviews.

Blue Heron Publishing
420 S.W. Washington Street
Suite 303
Portland, Oregon 97204
503.22.6841
info@blueheronpublishing.com
www.blueheronpublishing.com

ISBN 0-936085-47-9

Printed in the United States of America.

Other books by Ray Dreyfack

    Nonfiction

        Customers: How to Get Them, How to Serve Them, How to Keep Them
        Supervisor's Script Book
        Psychic Selling Strategies That Multiply Your Income
        Sure Fail, the Art of Mismanagement

    Fiction

        The Image Makers

Introduction

I could name any number of former freelance writers—some experienced, some not so experienced; some fairly competent, others super competent—whose matchless prose has been lost to posterity. These are either ex-writers who quit in frustration and went back to being plumbers, salespeople, and bartenders—or copouts who decided to follow new pursuits. Whatever the case, they are no longer self-employed as writers. If employed as writers by others, they can no longer write what they want, but must write what they are told to write. In some cases, it's a sad loss to society. In most cases it adds up to frustrated hopes and lifetime dreams down the drain.

The key question is: Why? Writers who choose freelance as a career are most commonly free spirits themselves. Creative idea generators, they rebel against restrictions and confinement, being told what to do, when and how to do it. So once, having courageously claimed the mantle of freedom and independence, why would they renounce it in favor of a lifestyle so much less attractive to them?

For a quick answer, try a five-letter word: *Money*! Currency, cash, coin of the realm, bank deposits and other financial assets. *Money*! The world's most popular brow-wrinkler and gray hair promoter. On a 9:00 to 5:00 job you know where next week's paycheck is coming from. Or you like to imagine you know. As a freelance you miss the regularity. But play it right and that loss loses significance. Actually, in today's volatile, downsize-happy marketplace, experience shows that the freelance who successfully squashes the insecurity bug will be miles ahead in the peace of mind department.

That's what this book is about. So let's squash away. But first you have to make sure you are qualified. Once you determine you have what it takes to be a successful freelance, squashing the anxiety bug will be as easy as writing a ten-word essay on why you love your mother.

What it takes in a nutshell

In a "nutshell," here's what it takes to succeed. Details—along with the critical how-to stuff—will come later, one fun-filled step at a time.

- Professional competence—not necessarily "great talent."
- Security savvy—the lowdown on what to write and for whom.
- Healthy outlook, psychologically, attitudinally.
- Ability to work alone.
- Realistic assessment of financial needs.
- Moral support from your family.
- Realistic assessment of lifestyle requirements.
- A burning desire to write and to publish.
- Knowhow—education, not necessarily formal.
- Tools of your trade—access to computer, word processor.
- Linkage to help and research sources.
- A yearning for knowledge and self-improvement.
- A strong sense of ethics and fair play.

If these requisites bring a frown to your face, wipe it off. There's no better time than now to get launched on your road to frown-free freelance independence. The good news is that every what-it-takes qualification listed above is developable. The best news is that you are just the writer who can do it if the desire and willingness to work hard to achieve it are strong enough.

Contents

	Introduction v
One	The bare bones essentials 1
Two	Specialize, specialize, specialize 15
Three	Farm where the soil is richest 30
Four	The rules of the selling game 45
Five	Spreading the word 59
Six	Cashing in on your computer 75
Seven	Should you write a book? 92
Eight	Love it, or leave it 107
Nine	To market, to market 122
Ten	Step-by-step from the ground up 136
	About the author 151

ONE
The bare bones essentials

As a cure for worrying, work is better than whiskey.

Thomas Edison

"Hey Jim, what's the matter, your face looks like new cement."

"I'm okay."

"Sure. Don't tell me you're not worried about something."

This dialog which I recall from a few years back was with a freelance writer friend. I finally coaxed the truth out of him. To say Jim was worried would be an understatement. His state of mind bordered on panic. Work assignments had been petering down which happens to the best of writers. On top of that, Jim's favorite editor, a primary source of income, had retired, shutting the tap when he needed it most.

No wonder he was worried. Married with two kids and a pregnant wife, Jim's income was vanishing while expenses kept rising. The proverbial well threatened to run dry with few prospects in sight to replenish it. Scary? Damn right! A year or so prior Jim had quit a job as an associate editor on a trade magazine to freelance full-time. It hadn't been a great job but it was steady.

"Biggest mistake I ever made," Jim groused.

Three months later he was back at the same kind of job he had left because of its frustration level and his dream of making it as an independent self-employed writer.

It still saddens me to think of it. I had made the same decision several years earlier: quitting a steady, dependable job to freelance. I regarded it then, and do now, as the smartest career move I ever made.

Why is it that one writer turns freelance only to become beset with panic level anxiety, while another writer goes the same route and is delighted and thrilled at the outcome? More important, what steps can one take to avoid the devastating effects of financial insecurity and at the same time cash in on the satisfactions and rewards of independence as a freelance writer? It is with these questions in mind that I decided to do this book.

First things first: how much security do you need?

Economic considerations aside, it would be hard to overstate the psychological importance of a steady, dependable income. The saddest thing about Jim's surrender is that during his year or so as a freelance he had obtained and successfully completed above-average-paying writing assignments. In short, Jim proved he was able to compete with the best of them, that his competence as a writer was first rate. Still, he couldn't survive. Not because he didn't have the skill to survive but because he wasn't up to the task psychologically. Financial insecurity did him in.

The reason is clear. We all have varying degrees of financial insecurity depending on our circumstances. Jim had failed to calculate the amount of security he needed and to address this requirement.

Facing this need squarely—objectively and subjectively—is step one in constructing a practical plan to become a psychologically secure freelance writer. Following through with an effective career strategy with this goal in mind—as spelled out in this book—is step two. Would that the implementation were as simple as the concept!

Consider your own situation. How much financial security do you need? It is a highly personal question whose answer differs from writer to writer. Here's what you must evaluate:

1. Your age.
2. Your health.
3. Your financial resources.
4. Current and projected debt obligations.
4. Your marital status.
5. If married, your spouse's income if any.
6. Your number of dependents.
7. Your ability to withstand psychologically the pressures of change.
8. Your reemployability if you leave your job.

Don't sell the numbers short

It boils down to arithmetic. You have to come up with a hard figure, an income level you can get by on given your personal situation. Obviously, a writer who's 26 years old and single is better positioned psychologically than a writer who's 40 years old with two or three children, one of whom will soon enter college. Similarly, the forty-year-old family man or woman with a bank balance of $200,000 and a spouse who is employed is better placed than the writer with $5,000 in the bank and a baby on the way.

In a nutshell, the less pressing your financial obligations at the time you decide to turn freelance, the lower the level of financial security you will need to keep you psychologically intact when you make the change. One writer may be comfortable with a projected annual income of $20,000; another may need $40,000 or more.

Does this mean that if your realistically calculated bottom line requirement is high a freelance career's not for you? Not at all. Not if you play your financial cards right.

> No matter how high your annual bottom line requirement, you can still achieve financial security as a freelance if you adhere to the strategies spelled out in this book! what's more, working for yourself, if you are relatively competent, you can still earn a great deal more than employed by someone else. And you can't be downsized.

One writer's experience

When I decided to go freelance full-time three decades ago, I set myself a double earnings standard. One was for the must-earn income I absolutely had to have to achieve a tolerable way of life for myself and my family. The other was my future projection—the much more ambitious income I was shooting for down the pike, my ultimate career goal. To accomplish this I could not afford to make the plunge prematurely.

> Read this twice if you are now employed and not yet a freelance. If you are a proven writer who has not yet made the leap into full-time freelancing this section is especially important for you.

When St. Augustine described patience as a "companion of wisdom" he must have had freelance writing in mind.

Unless you're in your late teens or early 20s and single with minimal financial obligations and in a position to quit your job and "take a shot" at going freelance, patience is the one virtue you cannot afford to sell short.

If you are burdened with financial responsibilities as most of us are, the best advice you could get is to avoid the deep water until it is thoroughly tested. View that must-earn annual income as a base. For example, let's say you're a proven writer who would like to go freelance with a must-earn annual income of $20,000. Assume further that you can count on $10,000 a year from interest, dividends, or other sources. That means you must earn the other $10,000 from freelance writing fees. It may not sound like much but that money won't come out of the blue.

That's pretty much the situation I faced when I decided to freelance back in the '60s. I had done considerable writing, had my fair share of rejections interspersed with some good hits and some valuable contacts, but few I could count on as repetitive. I was employed at a nonwriting job for a cosmetics company, my wife was a homemaker, and I had two young children to support. I can tell you that gives a guy something to think about.

From a financial standpoint I had a dependable job. But on the one hand, I didn't like what I was doing, and on the other, I had caught the writing bug. I was between the proverbial rock and a hard place.

I'd had some success as a nonfiction writer and had sold short stories to sports pulp magazines. Big deal, small income. I knew I could put words together and make them sell. But bills for everything from clothes and shelter to the kids' dental work and music lessons kept pouring in like rain through a leaky roof. Could I count on income from freelance writing to do the same? Too much of a gamble. At least at that point. When? That's where patience comes in.

Make a gradual transition

In making the switch from employee to self-employed freelance, exercising patience involves three simple rules.

1. Don't quit your job impulsively.
2. Turn out copy and develop contacts while still employed.
3. Ease gradually into a full-time freelance career.

If you have regularly recurrent financial obligations you can't afford to take the giant step until you have a comfortable number of repeat freelance assignments. Any other course automatically generates financial insecurity, wipes you out psychologically, and explains why so many writers chicken out after freelancing a short period of time.

No one said it was easy. Working full-time and extending your work week 10 or 15 hours writing evenings and weekends can be a grind. Is it worth it? It depends how much you want the pot of shekels at the end. As my own and a host of other writers' experiences show it is an anxiety-free way to develop the sources you will need to achieve financial security as a freelance. You will build up a cash reserve while doing it, and if you follow the guidelines spelled out in this book, it needn't take you that long.

The idea, after developing a few sources of dependably repetitive freelance writing assignments—two or three may be all you need to get rolling—is to ease gradually into a freelance writing career. At the outset, when I decided to make the switch, I spent less than a year developing three contacts I could depend on for steady ongoing assignments. Slow and steady! Cliché or not, honor it. For me the cash-in was promising from the outset.

1. Regular monthly features for a secondary magazine.
2. Regular contributions for a bimonthly newsletter.
3. Regular monthly booklets for a mail order marketer.

Fulfilling these assignments took less than one week per month and yielded 30% of my must-have income. Before leaving my full-time employer I was able to land a part-time job (2 days a week) with a small public relations firm. By then I was taking in 120% of my must-earn income. (About 80% of my prior full-time nonwriting job). My work consisted solely of writing and I still had several free hours per month in which to continue expanding my sources and building my income. On top of that, I was diversifying and solidifying my experience. I was on my way.

Try part-time work en route to full-time independence

In large cities especially, thousands of small firms are unable to hire full-time employees and are in the market for part-time help. Writers included; maybe writers especially. To avoid the transition shock of suddenly finding yourself bereft of the steady income to which you're accustomed, the part-time route can be a smart one to take on the road to financial security as a full-time freelance.

If you have proven writing ability as either a freelance or job holder, so much the better. Search hard enough—following the proven successful tips in this book—and the odds are high you will find yourself a part-time job as a writer. Combined with a couple or three regular sources, you will be well on the way to financial independence before you even make the final transition.

Keep in mind that change in itself can be traumatic and a career change one of the big shaker-uppers. Financially sound strategy is essential to cushion the shock. Developing regular sources of income is as strategically sound as you can get. No less sound is a transitional part-time writing job.

Such a move will not only help bankroll your venture. It will have the added plus of broadening and diversifying your writing experience as well as establishing what may turn out to be one of your best freelance contacts in years to come. The small PR firm, Richard R. Connaroe Associates, where I worked part-time after leaving my job, introduced me to the immensely profitable world of corporate writing—articles, speeches, brochures, company publications, you name it. More on this in Chapter 3. Working under Dick Connaroe, a bright light in this business, was an education in itself. And a year or so later when I made the full break to freelance work, Dick became my number one source. By this time I was almost as familiar with his clients and needs as he was.

It would be hard for me to overstate the value of Dick's training and encouragement.

Repetition—your security blanket

Just as financial security as an employee depends on a regular weekly or monthly paycheck, so does security as a freelance depend on regular repetitive fees. Repeated assignments you can count on from month to month constitute the security blanket you will need as a freelance to cover yourself and your family.

Freelance assignments? What kind? Where will they come from? How do you get them? This book is loaded with answers to these critical questions. The "how" will come later. For starters consider the following rundown.

Your local newspaper

Freelance Jeffery D. Zbar writes a weekly column that specializes in advertising and marketing. Werner Renberg does a weekly column on mutual funds. Gary Stein, billed as a local columnist for the Florida *Sun-Sentinel*, appears three times a week. Dave Joseph does a "Commentary" on sports. Marcia Pounds' column on "Business Strategies" appears every Sunday. You won't get rich writing for the local press, but it's a steady source of income.

Secondary magazines

Editors of hundreds of secondary publications, the ones you don't see on the newsstands, are hungry for contributions on subjects from A to Z. For decades I have been on the editorial staff of *The American Salesman and Supervision Magazine*, as has Bill Lissy with his fine column on labor law. Many such publications "pay in the dark" as the saying goes. But the checks appear with the regularity of the phone bill each month and constitute an important part of the freelance's financial base.

Trade journals

Many trade publications struggle with tight budgets for writers. The pay there is low, the need for regularly supplied material no less urgent. Several years ago I did rewrites for a printing and die stamping magazine, now defunct. Those small checks were most welcome when I needed them. Other trades, such as *Plant Engineering*, are highly successful with large circulations and prestigious advertisers. The fees here for specialized copy are respectable and in some cases generous. Billed as "Special Projects Editor," my biweekly column, "The Human Side of Engineering," has been running in *PE* for over 30 years. I could not speak too glowingly about the editors of this leading publication in its field and my treatment at their hands. Trades run the gamut from advertising and bottling to real estate and transportation. They constitute a wide open market for freelances, and a solid base when needed.

Newsletters

Name a subject from alabaster to zucchini and the odds are high you will find a newsletter that covers it. Here's a freelance market that offers not only steady income, but a chance to write about what grabs you most. Special expertise sells as we shall see. The writer who "knows his stuff" about aeronautics, electronics, precious stones, horses, criminology, or what have you, will find a warm reception from editors of specialized newsletters in these fields. If you haven't done it as yet, there is no time like now to get started becoming the house expert on any number of fields. Early on, I knew no more than the average person about corporate telephone service. But I became intrigued by the high cost of phone misuse in many organizations. I researched the subject, learned how to improve telephone service and save money that way, and developed consulting and corporate information sources. Before long I was contributing regularly to a newsletter titled *Better Business by Telephone.* This paid off when I needed it most. Later I cashed in on my years of management and supervisory experience and became a regular "stringer" supplying material for a half dozen or so newsletters published by Prentice-Hall and the National Foremen's Institute. When I acquired expertise in the field of customer service I started writing regularly for The Dartnell Corporation's group of newsletters on management, sales, and customer service. "Items" contributed to these publications usually paid $40 to $60 apiece—not so demeaning two or three decades ago—but I can recall sending off as many as 15 or 20 at a time. That adds up to money. With newsletters as my launching pad, I became an expert on customer service, even wound up doing a bestselling direct mail book on the subject. As my experience testifies, the newsletter world is one that is well worth exploring.

Direct mail publishers

Direct mail can be a rich field to mine for the freelance. Countless books, booklets, and newsletters, are shipped weekly this way. Here again your special expertise can pay off handsomely. For over two decades, I sold two or three booklets per month on subjects dealing with management, supervision, and sales to The Dartnell Corporation in Chicago. The compensation was a shade short of modest, but eventually I was able to turn out the articles so fast, mostly out of my own personal experience, and with a minimum of research, that they constituted a major part of my income and helped to bolster my sense of financial security.

The corporate world

Corporate writing is the plum orchard for freelances. The need for help is great and so is the potential reward. As we shall see in detail in Chapter 3, to mix a metaphor, the fattest cows in the pasture roam this terrain. For writers who compose speeches or ghost books and articles for high level executives fees in excess of $100 per hour are commonplace. Compensation for brochures, proposals, newsletters, and other projects for Fortune 500 companies—and lesser lights—can be heady as well. Before plucking the plums, however, a freelance must first earn credentials that impress the CEOs, VPs, public relations managers, personnel directors, and other execs who do the hiring. Ordinarily, unusual breaks excepted, freelances must inch their way to the Fortune 500 level a patient step at a time. One sure way to do this is to target as sources the many smaller companies that require writing assistance. Budgets for the most part may be tight, but depending on their needs, smaller companies can provide a steady stream of work.

Teach a course or two

Every freelance can boast at least one area of expertise: writing. For years, at the outset of my freelance career, I taught a course in business writing at the local adult school and had a great time doing it. The fee was less than respectable, but added threads to my security blanket nonetheless. In addition, if you held a responsible job for any length of time before becoming a writer, the skills and knowhow you acquired—technical or professional—may be of value to others. My prewriting career was in systems and data processing management. I spouted this expertise in courses at both the local adult school and New York University Management Institute. This steady source of income worked together with compensation from other outlets to add up to financial security. Many adult and community schools are interested in supplementing or expanding their curricula and are in the market for expertise of one kind or other. It's not likely the administration will approach you unless you're well known; the proposal will have to come from you. Submit a resume with a sexy description of your qualifications and the course you have in mind.

As a competent writer you should know just how to make your presentation sing.

Interact on the Internet

A whole chapter will be devoted to email, the World Wide Web, and the Internet as they affect the freelance. For the time being, keep in mind that the computer-based opportunities are exciting, in most cases free or low cost. In Florida

I am linked up with one provider (Icanect) for a modest monthly charge, and another (Seflin) the Southeast Florida Free Net. In the years ahead, spreading the word on the net about one's abilities and availability will constitute a must-do for writers who wish to expand both their contacts and horizons.

What about fiction?

That's a tough question. I consider fiction from two vantage points:

1. So far as earning a living is concerned no category of writing is harder for a freelance to sell than fiction. The short story market, never propitious, has all but dried up. The novel? From a financial perspective, unless yours is a well known name, the novel is a high risk venture. Time was you could send a book length fiction manuscript to an editor who would buy it if he or she liked it. Past tense except in rare cases. Today, most often, for an editor to even consider a novel the complete book must be submitted. I'm talking about months—or years—of work. On top of that, today's hot subject may be "off market" by the time the book is completed.

I've been through this mill, having been bitten by the fiction bug years after having become established as a successful nonfiction writer. It is a hard blow to take after spending months on a novel to be told the genre is no longer in demand. If that fails to discourage you, keep in mind that many larger publishers won't read a novel that hasn't been submitted by an agent. Finally, if your masterpiece does somehow get reviewed by an editor who likes it, prior to acceptance it must be reviewed again and again by accounting and marketing types who evaluate it with the cold detachment they would give a newly proposed plastic product and whose main objective is to knock down the advance.

2. Vantage point number two begs a disclaimer. I completed three novels in my career, not because this made any sense, but because I was mindlessly driven to do it. The first, and least impressive of the lot, I sold to a small paperback house, now defunct. My $1,000 advance (which came to about $2 per hour) was all the money I ever saw. My second novel, which I still

consider the best writing I ever did and which my agent liked, I couldn't sell because it was judged off-market by editors who reviewed it. Novel three, a more commercial effort, was also ruled off-market—too many suspense books of this kind now in the stores.

Having said all this, do I consider the countless hours devoted to fiction a waste of time? Not at all. For one thing, I indulged myself at a point in my life when financial security was no longer my goal. My kids were grown, with families of their own, and didn't need my help. So besides the fun of writing fiction, and it can be fun, what did I get out of it? A great deal. Most important, I learned how to fictionalize my nonfiction writing and make it more interesting with lively dialogue and added imagination in getting the message across. Having served my self-imposed apprenticeship as a writer of fiction, I think I am a much better writer of nonfiction today. I chalk up the novels I wrote as valuable—but costly—learning experiences.

Think _{Small} on Your Way to Thinking **Big**

If you are paying attention, by Chapter 2 you will probably be tired of hearing me say this, but unless you are already earning Big Bucks as a freelance, I can think of no counsel. I could cite any number of nonfiction writers who earn six-figure incomes as freelances. But only in rare cases does one catapult all at once into the big money. Most often this goal is reached a small patient step at a time. I can recall vividly the time when I could have papered my walls with rejection slips I got trying to break into magazines like *Esquire, The New Yorker,* and *Cosmo,* or attempting to sell book proposals to Simon & Schuster and Random House, before even having an agent, no less. The Slush Pile Kid, they could have called me. I learned the hard way that the biggest mistake a freelance could make is to go for the gravy before the meat is on the plate. Competition is as tough in writing as in manufacturing or retailing. Why pit yourself against thousands of writers instead of a handful? Almost all big bucks projects are booked by literary agents. It is hard to even get a reading without a good agent's guidance and contacts. And it's as hard to get a good agent as it is to sell a big bucks project without one.

So what's a freelance to do?

One more time:

Small first, **big** later.   *There, I said it again!*

Two points are worth keeping in mind:

1. If you're a qualified freelance, modest-paying assignments (corporate, newsletter, trades, etc.) are relatively easy to get—the competition factor. Considering the importance of continuity, keep in mind, too, that the more repeat assignments you get, the easier and *faster* they are to write.
2. A 2,000 word article on a familiar subject that pays $200 may take a fraction of the time needed to complete a 2,000 word article paying $800. Usually less research is involved, less editorial interaction, and rarely if ever a kill fee. Once expertise is acquired an article often all but writes itself.

Focus on the meat before you go for the gravy.

Cash in on your experience

How to cash in on your experience will be covered in depth in Chapter 2. But for the present here are some thoughts to consider.

Whatever job or jobs you held since coming out of high school or college, if you can also write, you may already have an area of expertise worth developing. I could cite a long list of writers, now profitably self-employed, who got started that way. Many writers specialize in one field or one industry.

What kind of work did you do before becoming a writer?

Did your experience include selling, accounting, engineering, or advertising? Did you work as a manager or supervisor? Were you an auto mechanic or machine operator? Did you work with computers? Were you a doctor, dentist, druggist, or mortician? Were you a professional athlete?

Reviewing my prewriting background, I worked a couple of years selling leather goods (both wholesale and retail). I served a long stint in supervision and data processing management. The first nonfiction piece I ever sold was to a data processing magazine. It paid $50 and the editor was happy to get more of the same because, as in most fields, experts who can write are hard to come by. In fact, the editor called *me* to solicit the story. I can still recall the heady experience, an editor actually soliciting me.

As a fledgling freelance most of my articles related to management and supervision, sales and marketing—fields of experience I knew inside out.

If financial security is your goal, it makes good economic sense to wed your expertise as a writer to your knowledge in other fields. There are innumerable accountants, salespeople, computer experts, lawyers, and insurance people in the marketplace. But very few who can also write. If you can do double duty as both expert and freelance your talents will be in demand, and you will eliminate the middleman, an employer who's probably paying you so much less than you deserve.

Spread the word

I know a writer who resigned an advertising job to go freelance. He started modestly enough, his first year out earning seventy percent of his former income. Today he's a millionaire, an entrepreneur who farms out as much work as he handles himself. He has a stable of freelance "stringers" on call and, like a literary agent, takes fifteen percent off the top of the fee. How does he do it?

The operational word is exposure. He spreads the word. Makes his presence, capabilities, and availability known throughout the marketplace. The "address" file in his computer contains hundreds of names:

- Writers
- Editors
- Publishers
- Literary Agents
- Public Relations Firms
- Corporate Executives
- Professional Associations

More important, they have *his* name, his phone number, and his email address. They're familiar with his personal page on the World Wide Web. They know what he can do and, if he can't do it himself, get others to do. When a CEO needs a good speech written yesterday the word is out that he's the guy to call. He can deliver in a pinch on short notice. His sources know this and are happy to pay for it.

"The trouble with most writers," this savvy businessman says, "is that they're too busy writing."

Right on! I should know because I've been too busy writing for years, too busy in my earlier years to take the time and effort needed to spread the word adequately, until I finally woke up to the importance of this for the freelance.

How to spread the word is the question. The answer is in any way and all ways that you can.

1. By word of mouth. Sending out tons of regular and email to all possible sources.
2. By making hundreds of phone calls offering your services and soliciting work.
3. By signing up a professional association or two like the American Society of Journalists and Authors and its second-to-none Writer's Referral service which brings together writers and clients.
4. By combing the want ads on a regular basis.
5. By subscribing to and interacting with specialized groups in your field of interest on the Internet.
6. By hooking up with a good literary agent once you feel qualified, submitting ideas on the one hand, while establishing periodic contact on the other to determine what is wanted and needed in the marketplace.
7. By trying to interest a literary agent or packager in your work. (More on this later.
8. By combing the pages of directories like the current "Writer's Market" which lists thousands of major and secondary sources for the freelance.
9. By setting up your own personal page on the World Wide Web.

IN A NUTSHELL: Blow your horn. Loud and clear.

TWO

Specialize, Specialize, Specialize

This is the age of the specialist.
Billy Rose

What applied decades ago applies even more strongly today, and to no one more so than the freelance. I know this from my own experience and from that of countless other writers. My specialization as a business writer, and sub-specializations within that main specialty—customer service, labor relations, speech writing, ghost writing, PR, etc.—have been and continue to be the most significant part of my income over the years. I've been asked: "What if you become bored with this specialization or that?" "What if a hot subject cools?" "What if editorial demand dries up?" Valid questions. But no one ever said that if you specialize in finance, let's say, or parenting, that you can't also specialize in raising pets or growing prize-winning roses. A specialist is an expert. In any field of endeavor you could name, the expert is in demand. And being in demand is what "achieving financial independence" is all about.

Another super plus of specialization is the opportunity it affords to do interesting and enjoyable work: What you want to do, not what you're told to do. It's no secret that when work is fun you tend to be better at it. If and when the fun fizzles, no problem. Switch to another specialization that appeals. In a lifetime of experience I have yet to meet an expert who did not enjoy being an expert. And if being an expert brings financial security to boot, what could be bad?

Take lead poisoning. Does the subject appeal to you? Maybe not. But it appeals to Brooklyn, New York, freelance Richard M. Stapleton. Lead poisoning, he realized, is of concern to millions of parents whose kids are exposed to it. So, having specialized in the subject, his informative book, *Lead Is a Silent Hazard*, continues to sell thousands of copies in stores and on the web. (We'll get to the web in Chapter 6.)

Says Stapleton, "For me recognition as an 'expert' is a neat ego boost, and certainly helps when pitching ideas." Personal commitment to the subject was for this committed freelance a prime motivator. Sales in the thousands isn't hay. But if you're out to make a bundle, he counsels, specialize in a subject where there's real money—meaning speaking and consultant fees, etc.

Specialization has treated New York City travel writer Paulette Cooper royally as well. She has done books and articles on subjects ranging from food and law to medical scandal and pets. "When I get bored," she says, "I go back to travel."

If you are a super specialist like Portland, Oregon, freelance Hal Higdon it would probably serve you well to set up your computer with folders (directories) that reflect your general specialization along with sub-folders reflecting specialties within that main category. Higdon is a sports enthusiast (his big seller, *Marathon*). On Hal's "directory" we find listings from running, tennis, basketball, to listings on health and fitness, all related to sports. Nor does that rule out other subject areas as well.

Facets galore

"Knowledge," says Blue Heron publisher Dennis Stovall, "is a little like a diamond. It is possible to cut a few facets or many." Each facet triggers new opportunities, fresh ideas, and new outlets for a multiple mileage bonanza.

Of course there are outlets and outlets. Specialize in Managing Alligator Farms and you'll sell your stuff to periodicals with a circulation of 46 for two cents a word, payable on publication. No way to get rich, let alone financially independent. The trick is to build bridges between your particular expertise and the readers and editors who have interest in it. The more players, the bigger the pot.

My agent tells me that parenting and religion/spirituality are hot subjects as of this writing, meaning that substantial numbers of readers and the editors who are trying to serve them plop down shekels to get the latest dope on the subject. Food specialization is popular but crowded. New twists and angles are needed. Sex always has and always will sell. So will aspects of marriage, winning the mate of your dreams. But, and this is a big but, tread warily when dealing with subjects where credentials are needed. If you're not a professional—doctor, psychologist, psychiatrist, scientist, etc.—either steer clear of the subject or hook up with a pro, if you can.

Florence Isaacs, who does a Q & A column for the American Society of Journalists and Authors (ASJA) newsletter, believes business and financial writing are well rated specialties, along with celebrity profiles, health and medical subjects. She ranks travel writing near the bottom of the heap although many travel scribes vehemently disagree. Which only proves that whatever you read or hear, nothing informs like your own personal experience. In her book, *Travel Writing in Fiction and Fact*, Jane Edwards draws on a wide range of examples to help writers understand how travel experiences can serve as the groundwork for their writing—and how travel writing can be made to pay off.

What is your particular interest? Are you a car buff? Pick up the latest copy of *Writer's Market* and turn to the section on Automotive and Motorcycle. More than two dozen markets are included—many more aren't listed. The world awaits your contributions.

The two main essentials

1. Choose Your Specialty(ies) Carefully!
2. Pick Your Markets with Special Care!

This section is worth stressing, and then stressing again. Keep in mind that your main goal—and the reason you are reading this book—is to persist and survive as a freelance economically and psychologically. They go hand in hand. You can't do one without the other.

Let's tackle number two first. Writers ask, "Ray, how come you don't write for the popular well known magazines? Isn't that where the big money is?" Granted, high circulation publications pay well. Top mags like *Reader's Digest, New Yorker, Woman's Day, Esquire, Good Housekeeping, Glamour, Family Circle, Playboy, Cosmopolitan, Parade, Parents,* and several others pay upward of $4,000 for articles. Not to be sneezed at.

So why do I sneeze? I don't exactly sneeze, but I blow my nose gingerly. I do write for magazines, major and secondary, but most often as corporate or PR assignments where my contract is with the client, not the publication.

The reason is a simple eleven-letter word—Competition! Excess competition creates psychological roadblocks.

"For some reason," says Blue Heron's Stovall, "most of us begin at the wrong end of the marketing spectrum. We submit our ideas, our manuscripts to the best paying, most prestigious national or regional publications and publishers. We compete with the best of the established pros. If you studied these writers' careers you would find that few, if any, started at the top or got there in one step."

If you studied my career you would find I'm no exception. When I think of the hours and postage wasted over the years I could… Forget it! What I could do is not printable.

My point is that depending on magazine assignments as a freelance—*unless you and the editor are on more or less equal professional footing*—makes you a highly vulnerable entrepreneur. Vulnerable to what? Okay, let's cite some examples.

In my experience with, and exposure to, freelance writing, a MAJOR CAREER BUSTER for writers I know who didn't make it was *attempting to buck the magazine market as a generalist*. Either that, or going the specialist route without proper forethought and planning. Do this and here's what you may be up against.

The freelance writer as punching bag

A frustrated writer once told me, "Remember Joe Louis? Well, sometimes I feel like Max after the Louis-Schmeling fight." I dub it *The Punching Bag Syndrome*. Here, from my files, is a rundown of case history freelance gripes and groans at "blows" endured at the hands of magazine editors and their penny-pinching employers.

The American Society of Journalists and Authors (ASJA), regarded as indispensable by many freelance writers, this one included, tracks and publishes writer abuses regularly in its information packed monthly newsletter. I make no pretense that writers who specialize wisely and well are immune to abuse. But punching bag hits are more the exception for successful specialists. They are well grounded and positioned to select the most solvent, reliable, and ethical markets. In short, when what you sell is in demand, you are in driver's seat mode.

Three of the most common complaints registered are: 1. Writers robbed of subsidiary rights to articles and other works, mostly electronic. 2. Writers hung up on fees by magazines that pay on publication. 3. Magazines that fold with writer-creditors left in the lurch, sometimes with substantial sums outstanding. This is just the tip of the iceberg. So tighten your seatbelt. Each of the following listed types of abuse has been repeated again and again. Nor will you be surprised to hear that in formulating the contracts and policies that trigger the complaints corporate lawyers and accountants almost invariably get into the act. Editors, for the most part, are the good guys, but too often beholden to their penny pinching bosses.

The Security Busters

- Writer's article, somewhat revised, appeared after submission and rejection under another writer's byline.
- Rightful fee finally collected, but only after a costly and time-consuming court battle.
- Article accepted, then returned with new specs and unreasonably long revisions after new editor took over. Fee increase request rejected.
- Payment finally received 8 months after submission, 6 months after acceptance, and 2 months after publication from magazine that "pays on acceptance."
- Query response from major magazine took 8 months. Article accepted with fee paid months after publication following repeated calls and correspondence. Three editorial changes during this period. Casual apology stated, "So sorry, records lost by payables department.
- Editor who "loved" article idea was replaced. Correspondence with new editor dragged on for months until idea was judged "no longer timely."
- Article rejected, then seen almost in its entirety on the web.
- CD-ROM reuse of article uncompensated. Time-consuming calls and correspondence to make amends.
- Unauthorized and uncompensated use of a published article in a sister publication.
- Late payment with "bill lost" response to inquiry. Bill resubmitted with "bill lost" response repeated. Bureaucracy reigns.
- Major magazine insists on unlimited and uncompensated re-

use of material in domestic and foreign editions.
- Lawyerly work-for-hire (we'll talk about this later) new policy deprives writer of copyright and requires uncompensated re-use of material.
- Recipes excerpted from food article and published elsewhere with no payment to author.
- Material sold off to a syndicate with profits hogged by the magazine.

Does all this imply that magazine editors and publishers are a bunch of greedy finaglers. Not at all! Several get high marks from ASJA and other writers' organizations. In addition to which, bureaucratic screw-ups do account for some of the abuse. But sadly as well, too often lawyers and accountants are paid big bucks to fatten corporate coffers by depriving authors, eager to see their brain children spawned, of fair return on their efforts.

Nor does this, for the most part, apply to the overwhelming majority of corporate publications—company periodicals of one kind or another—which with rare exceptions, as we shall see in Chapter 3—are very much on the up and up. But the reality is that too many abusers and their writer-insensitive policy-making committees are out there in force, and working hard to force compliance with unjust and unreasonable stipulations and provisions.

Fighting back

What conclusions can we draw from all this? Does it rule out magazine sales as a viable source of income for the freelance in search of long range financial security? Absolutely not! It would be security mayhem to ignore the reality that so many of the billions of words written each year do appear in magazines of one kind or another. So what's a poor writer to do? How do you cash in on the income from magazine sales and at the same time avoid being victimized by the all too frequent abuses?

The trick is to qualify as the kind of writer who doesn't get stomped on?
Unfortunately, only a relatively small number of freelances in the market today fill this bill, and we're not necessarily talking about writing ability. You may be a highly competent writer and still beat your gums if you grind out submissions to magazine slush piles without having the reputation and credentials that make it profitable to do so. The reasons are clear:

- First and second level pubs get thousands of queries and proposals each week.
- Only a relative handful of the great mass of writers who are out there competing for the choice assignments are the elites who nail them. If you are a privileged member of this group, more power to you; put down this book and pick up a good novel.
- Assuming you are not one of The Chosen, your humble submissions are likely to be read by a low-paid, fresh out of college grunt with as much experience and ability to evaluate your brilliant brainchild as your mother-in-law's parrot. That is, assuming it wasn't rejected out of hand to begin with because it wasn't submitted by a literary agent.
- As the ASJA Newsletter reports regularly, writers in the know are aware that magazine editors change faster than leaves in October.
- As is also made clear in the Newsletter, secondary magazines, and some not so secondary, fold faster than envelope inserts in the mail department.
- Finally, if you check the masthead of many publications you will note that often some if not most articles and features are penned not by freelances but by staffers.

Okay, that's the bad news. The good news is that you *can* Achieve Financial Independence as a Freelance—even become outrageously wealthy—and submit to magazines or not as you wish *if* you heed these four simple essentials:

1. Proceed a slow and sensible step at a time.
2. Tailor your specialization(s) to need and demand.
3. Don't compete with elites unless you are an elite yourself.
4. Stand up aggressively for your rights as a professional.

Objective one, if you're not an elite, is to sidestep the slush pile at major magazine and book publishing companies. Savvy specialists accomplish this deftly. Although ASJA lists over 200 magazines that pay from $800 to upwards of $4,000 for articles, in my experience dating back decades, I have found that I could earn more per hour on a piece that paid $300 or $400 than on many that paid in the thousands. You don't have to be a math wiz to calculate the return on an 800-word article paying $300 that you knock off in a day or less, versus a 4,000-word article paying $3,000 that took more than two weeks to research, write, and revise. More per hour is what financial independence is all about, because as a freelance what you sell most is your time.

The savvy specialist and disabuse

A brief word on "fighting back." Three savvy freelances I know:

1. Having committed to do a magazine article for $3,000, the contract deprived the writer of electronic and other rights to the piece. He protested and was told, "Sorry, that's our policy." The writer said, "In that case, no deal." The editor capitulated. The lost rights provision was removed from the contract.
2. The editor and writer negotiated back and forth on an article's price. When the editor held firm at $2,500 the writer backed out on the deal. "Hold on a minute," the editor said over the phone. When he returned, the writer's $3,000 asking price was approved.
3. A $1,500 price was agreed upon at the outset. When the editor made word length and other changes requiring unanticipated time and effort, the writer demanded an additional $500 for the extra work. The editor refused. The writer held firm for the $500 or else. He won out in the end.

These examples speak for themselves. As any experienced freelance could confirm, magazine empires do indeed have their policies with regard to price, rights, and everything else. But savvy freelances have their policies as well. Moral of the story: If the editor wants what you have to give, badly enough, corporate policy can be bent and stretched if need be. It happens time and again.

The pygmy advantage

As a freelance for which career level do you qualify?

>   Top Level—Well established in your field and in a position to negotiate with editors on a more or less equal footing.
>   Mid Level—Getting established, achieving credentials and recog-

nition, but not yet a well known and important name in your field.

Low Level—Not many notches in your literary belt as yet. You have a long hard road ahead of you—which this book will endeavor to make easier.

No one I ever knew was too smart or successful to cash in on new knowledge and ideas. As a Top Level, you will find many tips, short cuts, and money-savers throughout this book that will hopefully add to the success you already achieved

Mid or Low Level, The Pygmy Advantage advocates the business-building and psychological values of going after low-paying assignments before (or at the same time as) shooting for the more lucrative gigs. In a nutshell: (one more time) Start SMALL to grow BIG!

Most advantageously: Try to establish a *financial base* of dependable repetitive assignments, however modest they may be, that will constitute a steady fixed percentage of your freelance writing income. In my years of experience, an important reality of freelance life I learned early on is that after a while regularly repeated assignments are completed so quickly they end up being quite profitable. Also, as you become more and more of a specialist, less and less research time will be needed. Long time specialists' primary research source rests right atop their shoulders. As exemplified by this book, 90 percent of the goodies disclosed are right from out of my own fuzzy head.

Turning back the clock three or four decades, I recall several relatively low-paid assignments as a specialist in various aspects of business and management that added up to more than half the income needed for myself and my family, and consumed less than half my working time. This included such items as management and supervision booklets for a mail order publisher, newsletter material for three different publishers, employee rack booklets, monthly column material for supervision and sales magazines. This solid, dependable base kept the worry wolf from my door for decades and never allowed the ugly beast to return.

The regionals

Special thanks to my publisher, Dennis Stovall, for his thoughts and insights contained in this important section.

Stovall recommends the regional (modest income) approach to getting published as an excellent path to survival and growth. Here are some of the reasons:

- I don't care how many books on writing you read, nothing will teach you how to write faster or more effectively than the time you spend at the keyboard. Get all the experience you can as quickly as you can. This is guaranteed to boost you from Low Level to Mid Level, and from Mid Level to Top Level. If you are already Top Level, it will push you higher up on the summit. More writing is the key to better writing. Better writing commands the markets in every genre. Ten years ago I thought I was a pretty good writer. I think I'm a better writer today because I wrote my heart out during the past decade.
- If you set your sights on selling to editors with whom you have the best chance—instead of harboring fantasies of appearing on Larry King or the Tonight Show—you will get more instructive feedback. If the piece is rejected, you'll have a better chance of learning why, and learning what it will take to get the next piece accepted.
- Credentials sell. Selling to the regionals, you gain not only experience, but clips and self-confidence. Keep in mind the Pygmy Advantage. In my own early experience specializing in various aspects of business and management, I gradually progressed from secondary markets which paid peanuts to prestigious markets which paid imported macadamia nuts. How you market yourself, as you will see, is a key success ingredient in this business. Editors don't like risk if they can avoid it. Before taking a chance on an unknown writer, they want to know what he or she has written before. Clips, clips, clips. Pygmy style—from small to big.
- Although Dennis Stovall, headquartered in Oregon, cites examples from the Pacific Northwest, the same opportunities exist everywhere. If you scan titles on the newsstand, library, or in your favorite bookstore, you are only scratching the surface. Most regionals cannot be reached through traditional outlets. Trade associations, hobbyists, academics, scientific, military, and

other specialized groups publish constantly but you won't find their publications through conventional sources. Special libraries typically provide the only access most of us have to this special world of publishing. Some libraries and booksellers have lists of regional publishers and publications. You have to get out there and dig.

The nuts and bolts of specialization

It is simple common sense that expertise sells. Whether the need involved relates to your car, your health, house hunting, or whatever, if you have your sights set straight you will seek out a specialist to guide you to the best possible deal. Editors are no different. In an effort to minimize risk, they will almost invariably place their bets on the expert. The problem for the freelance, of course, is to qualify as an expert. The challenge is how to achieve this financial independence-guaranteeing objective.

No problem!

> The crucial point to keep in mind is that:
> Every expert was at the outset an amateur!

> The key question to confront is:
> How do you make the transition from novice to specialist?

Read on.

Experience

Most writers are experts and often do not even know it. Or if they do they underrate the extent of their expertise. Or they make no effort to evaluate the money-making potential of their expertise.

Most of us already possess expertise that may or may not be marketable. My own experience is not unusual. Prior to going freelance full-time, my stints as an employee dating back to my twenties include:

1. Leather goods salesman, wholesale and retail.
2. Data processing operator—Army and private enterprise.
3. Data processing supervisor.

4. Data processing manager.
5. Systems director.

Get the picture? My two years of sales experience armed me with selling and marketing knowhow. My data processing experience introduced me to the world of punch card accounting, and from there to computers. Supervising and managing people and procedures over the years gave me insights into motivational techniques and strategies, labor relations, and guiding and directing employees with corporate as well as individual goals in mind. It didn't occur to me at the time, but I was slowly becoming an expert, in management in particular.

Once I determined that my freelance career would be full-time, my specializations and sub-specs blossomed into full bloom. At the outset I penned articles on data processing, supervision, sales, and management for low-paying magazines. A data processing magazine editor in particular, hungry for material and hard put to find people with data processing expertise who could also write, purchased everything I wrote.

Step by step over the years, I upgraded my markets while—Pygmy style—continuing to sell to the low-paying steadies because it was income that would always be there. Once I started to hit *Nation's Business* regularly, I knew I was on my way. Specialization, as much as any other factor, helped me Achieve Financial Security as a Freelance Writer with frosting on the cake to boot. Out of my sales and marketing expertise emerged my mail order bestseller Management Guide for The Dartnell Corporation: *Customers: How to Get Them, How to Serve Them, How to Keep Them*. Out of my supervisory experience came my mail order bestseller, *Supervisor's Script Book*, for Prentice-Hall. Out of my managerial experience came my profitable monthly column, "The Human side of Engineering," for the wonderful people at *Plant Engineering* magazine, a valuable security blanket for decades. Were it not for my varied and assorted specializations I would still be a corporate vassal. Ykhh.

Sit down and compile a list of your own working and living experience. Did you teach, manage, sell, work in a lab, repair cars, serve as a therapist, doctor, lawyer, or Indian Chief?

As a parent have you developed interesting ideas and theories relative to bringing up children? As a cook, have you dreamed up lip-smacking recipes or health-building menus? Publications exist that cover all of these topics and more. Check them out. Your experience may be a freelance's gold mine.

Plunge fearlessly into the fray

A lesson I learned more than thirty years ago from former employer, mentor, associate, and friend, Public Relations savant Richard R. Conarroe, has served me well ever since. Dick's PR clients came to him from time to time with assignments on subjects remotely alien to his experience. Still, I have never known him to turn down a challenge because of his lack of expertise. Some gigs he would turn over to me.

When he came to me with the task of writing a brochure designed to sell a world class seagoing yawl, The Bolero, my instinctive response was: "What do I know about yachts and how to sell them? The mere idea made me seasick." Working for Dick, I learned not to voice such negative thoughts. I did the brochure and the yawl was sold. I suddenly knew something about boats which I have long since forgotten, but my "expertise" served me well at the time.

One of the most challenging assignments I ever fulfilled was the penning of an article for *Harvard Business Review* on how to acquire a company. The client, Rockwell Manufacturing Co., the bylined author, Willard (Al) Rockwell. The corporate objective: Acquisition by Rockwell, a relative midget, of North American Aviation, an industry giant. The article, when published by *HBR*, had been credited by savants as a key factor in the midget's successful, and highly unconventional, acquisition of the giant. Within time, as you know, the company became known as North American Rockwell, with Al Rockwell at the helm. And I became something of an expert on mergers and acquisitions.

The point is clear. Every expert starts out as an amateur. What did I know about acquiring a company? Zilch! No matter. In today's information surfeited world, what you don't know, you find out. I interviewed Al Rockwell and a half dozen or so of his top aides, and before I knew it, I was a "specialist" on the fine corporate art of merger and acquisition. Anyone can become an expert. All you have to do is take the plunge. Thanks, Dick, for helping to instill that philosophy.

Link with an expert

You don't have to be an expert to write with expertise on most subjects. Say you have an opportunity to do an article on preventing the extinction of dolphins or manatees in a particular area. What qualifies you to handle this assignment? Apart from a little chutzpah, nada or less. But be not deterred.

All you have to do is set up an interview for a friendly, quiet chat with a professional in the field. At most it may cost you a lunch.

Is pinning down an expert for an interview too great an imposition? Usually not. Most experts are enthusiastic about their area of interest—which helped them evolve into experts—and once wound up are hard to stop. If what you plan to write will in some way be useful and instructive as it relates to their subject, they will be happy to make their own contribution. Finally, experts thrive on recognition and credit. Apply fair attribution in your article, and writer-friendly experts will be glad to cooperate.

A writer I know was invited to do a brochure for the American Petroleum Industry, completely outside his realm of expertise. Overcoming his initial what-do-I-know-about-that reluctance, he began to interview experts in the field. "By the time I was finished," he said, "I had enough material for a book." This in a nutshell is one way specialization is born.

Another writer I once worked with has developed a set of jargon dictionaries, tailored to fields of interest he covers. He reviews the appropriate notebook prior to client meetings and interviews.

Write a book

Was I an expert on the family and health benefits of walking, serving customers, supervising employees, Japanese management, insurance industry selling, corporate social responsibility, just for starters? Absolutely not! Nonetheless I wrote published books on these subjects and more, twenty-seven in all. I thus became an overnight expert twenty-seven times over. Well, not exactly. Certainly not in depth. Some subjects tackled decades ago, Japanese management, for example, are only dimly remembered. To tackle this subject I would have to reeducate myself.

But the point is that image counts for much in this writing game. The perception, valid or not, that the freelance who wrote a book is by virtue of that action an expert, is automatically assumed, not only by friends and neighbors, but by editors as well.

Are you the editor of an environmental magazine working on an issue that should have been closed yesterday, but can't be closed until you find a freelance qualified to provide you with a quick feature story on lead poisoning? The man to call is Dick Stapleton whose book, *Lead Is a Silent Hazard*, rates him as the source to access on this subject.

Are you the editor of a money magazine forced to reject an article on managing your finances because it didn't hit the mark? The lady to call is Grace Weinstein whose books, *Children & Money: A Parent's Guide,* and more recently, *Men, Women & Money: New Roles, New Rules,* establish her as a foremost expert in the field. Today Grace writes innumerable articles on all aspects of personal finance. She's a regular columnist for *Investor's Business Daily,* and is also the editor of a monthly newsletter called *Money Matters.* All this in addition to her frequent corporate assignments. Moral of the story: Books are more than stepping stones; they are stepping career ladders.

Multiple mileage

A major reason I never had to deal with insecurity, says six-figure income freelance John "Jack" Behrens of Clinton, New York, is that "I acquired a plan for reusing salable ideas." Once you specialize you can use and sell the same material—with a new twist, a new slant, a new format—over and over again.

I couldn't begin to count the number of spin-offs I enjoyed after I researched and wrote my bestselling book on customer service. Articles, newsletter submissions, booklets—you name it. Sometimes, as in Grace Weinstein's experience, a book grows out of magazine or newspaper articles. Sometimes, as with the fallout from my customer book, it happens the other way around. Whatever the case, multiple mileage means more, easier, and faster income than when breaking new ground. The savvy freelance does both.

Do you want to specialize but don't know how or where? Consider writing a book. If you're not a specialist at the outset, you will be one when you're done.

THREE

Farm where the soil is richest

To be clever enough to get a great deal of money, one must be stupid enough to want it.

G. K. Chesterton

Okay, so call me stupid. Stupid enough in any case as a freelance to avoid barren ground if I can confine my digging where the soil is most fertile.

In my long experience, corporate writing is the Nile Valley of freelance terrain. Innumerable writers I know and have contacted agree. As New Jersey-based Alan Caruba, founder of The Boring Institute, puts it: "Corporate writing pays better than just about any other form of professional writing." Unless your name happens to be John Grisham, Elmore Leonard, Frank McCort, Pat Conrad, or one of those guys.

"Pays better" is one of the two most important reasons to consider—and reconsider—corporate work if your goal is to Achieve Financial Independence as a Freelance Writer. Reason number two is the treatment you get.

As New York City's Richard Blodgett states the case: "In my experience, corporations—especially larger corporations—treat writers who conduct themselves as professionals with the respect that professionals deserve."

Blodgett cites two examples. "When I wrote a corporate history for an insurance company, I was booked into top-line hotels while visiting offices across the U.S. to conduct interviews. I was taken to dinner by a local executive in each of the cities I visited. When the book was published, the CEO invited me to lunch and presented me with a china bowl from Tiffany as a thank-you.

"On another assignment, while visiting a client in Wisconsin, my flight home from Milwaukee was fogged in. To make sure I got home that night, the company hired a limousine to take me to Chicago and had a plane ticket waiting for me at the airport. I didn't even ask that they do this. They just went out of their way to treat me well."

My own experience echoes Dick's. On an assignment from North American Rockwell to cover the Apollo moon landing for a *Harvard Business Review* article, I was flown to Oklahoma and California, put up in the finest hotels, taken on grand tours of the space facilities, and introduced to Astronaut Buzz Aldrin and other high flyers. Heady stuff, not to mention the payment which was also big time. Typical from start to finish.

When, for three years running, I wrote recruitment brochures for one of the Big Eight accounting firms, I was treated royally while conducting interviews in several U.S. cities. Wined and dined, best hotels, VIP service all the way. From the sensible and well calculated corporate perspective: The better you treat people who work for you, the more effort they will expend on your behalf, the more inspired they will be to perform. As any good consultant could confirm, it works.

Some writers, Blodgett told me, view corporate writing as boring. In my experience, no way! Boring? The Apollo assignment was one of the most exciting I have been on. Ditto for the corporate history I did for Sperry & Hutchinson, covering the traumatic battle between S&H and A&P-Safeway in the superchain's efforts to do away with Green Stamps. High drama, high pay.

Doing it

So, as a financial independence achiever to be, how do you cash in on this corporate writing bonanza? No one said it was easy. But in this writer's experience it is definitely doable.

The Triple C Formula features:

1. Contacts
2. Clips
3. Credentials

Accumulate credentials one clip at a time. If you are starting from scratch or nearby, keep the oft repeated admonition in mind:

Start SMALL to grow BIG!

Realistically, you won't arrive at Bonanzaville before hitting the local stops along the way. If you're new at the game, this means progressing from small companies and small pay, to midsize organizations and modest pay, en route to large corporations and big pay. It could take months, it could take years, depending on how much hard time, hard effort, and hard thought you invest in the enterprise. In my case, it took me about ten years or so before I started hitting the big time.

More years ago than I care to remember, a friend who owned a small electronics firm asked me do a four-page annual report for distribution to his eighty or so shareholders. I obliged, and charged him $175 for about two days' work—in contrast to the $1,200 fee a PR agency had quoted. I continued doing this as a favor for a number of years. From this humble beginning developed annual report assignments from larger companies for more respectable fees. A step at a time, a clip at a time, a credential at a time. But it all starts with a contact.

Another port of entry is via the regional route. Concord, California, freelance Donna Albrecht, whose expertise includes public relations, copywriting and advertorials, was specializing in real estate writing for regional publications when PR people in the area noticed her work and liked it. This led to a regular column for a real estate firm and, subsequently, ghostwriting for local Realtors who wanted articles published in the industry national trade journal.

More than a client

Establish a good, mutually profitable working relationship with a client and you win more than a client. You win a friend and a years long source of dependable income.

My initial acquaintanceship with Robert E. Levinson was a couple of decades ago, when, as a client of Dick Conarroe's PR agency, he was CEO of Cincinnati's Steelcraft Manufacturing Co., a family-owned business and the nation's largest producer of metal doors.

Over the course of the years I did two books for Bob, several speeches, and scores of articles published in general and business magazines, and I am currently working with him on a third book. Years later, when Dick sold his PR firm, Bob contacted me on numerous occasions when he had PR projects in mind. The relationship continued even after Steelcraft was sold to American Standard Corporation where Bob functioned as that corporate giant's marketing vice president for two or three years. During this stint I did articles and speeches for him with various image-building goals in mind. By this time, Bob was far more than a client; he was a good friend to me and my family.

When he was downsized from American Standard, Bob Levinson, one of the most astute businessmen I ever knew, was well prepared for the ax. The hotel business had always intrigued him and in his sixties by now, he purchased a Holiday Inn in South Florida. Masterful at the art of customer service, the hotel flourished, and he bought another Holiday Inn in Pompano Beach followed by a Sheraton in Boca Raton.

One February, working with Bob on a book, I learned that my son Ken, a writer living in France, had made plans to come to the U.S. on a combined business/vacation trip. By that time I was living and working in South Florida. Ken was prepared to spend a bundle to lodge his family of five. It occurred to me that the $3,000+ expense for a two-week stay might not be necessary.

I gave Bob Levinson a call and proposed a deal: Put up my son and his family in your Holiday Inn on the ocean, and I'll provide an equivalent amount of writing service on a barter arrangement. Bob didn't have to think twice. "Done," he replied. I did my best to give him more than the equivalent, and Ken and his family enjoyed a vacation more luxurious than what he could have afforded at the time.

Moral of the story: When you expand a client relationship beyond service to friendship, all kinds of by-product benefits tend to develop.

Another valuable friendship, originating with my part-time employment in Richard R. Conarroe & Associates, is the one I developed with Dick. As I mentioned, I continued working for and with Dick over the years. I even went into business with him at one point as an editor and copublisher of a newsletter titled *Profit Improvement News,* which seemed promising for a while but eventually fizzled. Nonetheless, our friendship never fizzled at social get-togethers, on the tennis court, and by telephone and email.

The point makes itself. Friendship is spawned out of things like helpfulness, outstanding service, and ethical professional relationship. Executives like Bob Levinson and Dick Conarroe need guys like me. And heaven knows that as a freelance who values his independence, I need guys like them.

All it takes is one contact

Early on in my career I was writing customer service articles for management, supervision, and office publications. I had plenty material in the storage vault between my neck and my scalp from my work as a manager. But experience taught me that quoting authoritative sources, their counsel and experience, will enhance any piece. In most—but not all—cases, a primary gateway to good corporate quotes is a well reputed public relations firm.

Making contacts works two ways. Sometimes exposure to your work generates a hit; other times you take the initiative. The more aggressively you seek contacts, the more contacts develop.

PR firms are usually ready, willing, and able to cooperate with writers, freelance or otherwise, in their quest for material. Their motivation is not necessarily altruistic. Like any other consultant, a primary goal of red-blooded PR account execs is to expand and perpetual client billings. Understandably, corporate clients want to know what they are getting and what they can expect to get for their money. Thus, periodic progress reports are mandated. The writer who seeks information for an article being written for a magazine or newspaper, for example, often winds up as an item on the agency's client report, something like the following:

> Writer inquiry. Anecdotal experience and quotes provided for freelance Ray Dreyfack who is doing an article for *Sky Magazine*.

On the one hand, this indicates that the PR firm is busy working on the client's behalf. On the other hand, it indicates that the agency is known to writers as a reliable source of material. Finally, it cites the interview experience—sometimes with the PR account exec, other times with a designated client executive—as yet another opportunity for print, air, or electronic exposure generated by the agency. An aid toward the ultimate goal of billing perpetuation.

Get the picture? In a nutshell, PR heads and account executives are writer-friendly people. From the freelance's perspective—checking the Triple C Formula listed above—it is apparent that touching base as often as possible with PR people constitutes a double-edged achievement tool. It provides information when needed while establishing contacts in the field. On top of that, the PR contact itself can be of value as an assignment-generating tool. Busy public relations agencies often find themselves in a scheduling bind.

They fall behind in writing press releases. They have feature stories to do and find themselves shorthanded. Vacation time finds them with gaps that need to be filled. What better filler than you?

What good are contacts? Contacts are like cucumbers. Do one planting, and they grow like crazy. From contacts develop assignments and referrals. In the freelance business it's what you know and who you know. Establish a contact and there's no telling when, where, or how it will bear fruit or by what serendipity a chain reaction will take off.

"How I got into corporate writing," Palm Springs, California freelance Warren Jamison told me, "is a shaggy dog story." Several years ago Jamison contacted a book packager with an idea. Nothing came of it. But the packager had gone to school with a woman who became a literary agent. One day she asked if he knew someone qualified to do a book for a Florida corporation. The packager dug out Jamison's list of book credits, was impressed, and recommended him for the project. Result, he wound up doing three well compensated books for the Florida company.

Contact is a magic word. The more contacts you make, the more likely you are to be contacted. If the business people are in the field of your choice, so much the better.

In 1986 a consultant friend of New York freelance Gary Stern asked him if he would be interested in editing an in-house newsletter for a money-center bank. Sniffing an opportunity for repetitive work, Stern agreed to be interviewed. Today, fourteen years later, he is still doing the newsletter. In the process he learned the business from A to Z.

The pricing game

Writing for magazines, newspapers, and book publishers, freelances usually have a fair idea of the fee ranges involved. Writing corporate stuff is a whole different soccer game. ASJA Q&A columnist Florence Isaacs was asked about the going rates for ghostwriting a book. Much if not most ghostwriting is assigned by corporate PR and other departments. The fee is dictated by the situation involved, Isaacs replied. Top ghostwriters for books command six figure fees. Rates range all over the place depending on the size of the company, the hierarchical level of the bylined executive, the status and reputation of the writer, the client's publishing and distribution objectives, the estimated time and effort involved, the number of interviews and locations involved.

"Whatever the fee," says Isaacs, "it should be more than it would be were your name on the book or article."

"How much should I charge?" is a perpetual freelance's dilemma. Sometimes a very pleasant dilemma.

There is no set fee I could suggest or recommend. The freelance, in my experience, has to find a compromise with such factors as fair market value, what the prospective client can afford to pay, how much in the writer's opinion his or he time is worth, and what the traffic will bear. In some cases, the contracting executive will specify the fee that the client will pay. If you feel you can negotiate for more without jeopardizing the assignment, you do so. If not, you agree on the stipulated price.

Other times the client will want to know what the project will cost. A concern shared by all executives is that in the case of an open ended arrangement the fee might be prohibitively high. For this reason I make it my business to put the client at ease early on. I never leave the price hanging. The way to do this is with a from-and-to stipulation. I quote a minimum—say $2,000—and a maximum—say $3,000. Typically, the price I bid is midway in-between. The psychological advantage is obvious. The client executive knows the fee can't go above the budgeted or authorized limit. In charging less than the maximum when I could have charged more, the client has the perception that I'm a fair minded writer—which I am.

Gain in-depth knowledge of your clients

One of the best decisions I ever made was, when I made the final break as an employee to ease my way into freelance work, was the arrangement to work two days a week for Richard Conarroe & Associates, a small, up-and-coming New York City-based PR firm. The main part of my job consisted of corporate writing. Considering that I had no image or reputation at the time, and was still short of experience, the modest fee I received more than satisfied my need for steady income and stability while I was learning my trade.

Within a year or so I was sufficiently indoctrinated to have achieved a level of financial independence, and wound up the two-day-a-week arrangement to venture full-time on my own. During this period I had become an asset to Dick and had gained account executive status on some of his corporate accounts. I continued as a "stringer" for years following my part-time stint. For one thing, I had come to know the clients almost as well as if I would had been employed by them. For another I had earned the respect and trust of both Dick and his clients. A short and patient step at a time.

Here's one of the best corporate slogans I ever saw:

> If the customer doesn't succeed, neither do you.

Getting to understand your clients' needs and profit objectives is a key factor in establishing a relationship you can count on for years. With Dick I was included in client-agency meetings, sometimes with Dick present, other times as the sole agency participant. I was in on the planning and organization of work projects and goals. In my mind, though self-employed, I functioned as an employee of both client and agency with the responsibility to serve each profitably. My compensation and independence were climbing, along with the number of contacts in my Business Opportunities File.

Most corporate executives can't write their way out of a cellophane wrapper. Corporations employ bright managers, scientists, engineers, financial planners, marketing mavens, and negotiators. But when it comes to communicating, more often than not they fall short. Those who are literate and articulate are too busy to write the articles, speeches, brochures, and press releases they need to get the message across. And in many cases, staff employees bureaucratized into PR, public affairs, marketing, customer relations, advertising, and other departments are qualified to grind out routine press releases, but lack the sophistication, imagination, and wider experience needed to handle the more challenging assignments.

This is all to the freelance's advantage. Thus the experienced freelance who, in addition to writing skills, has gained insights into the client's business and communications needs becomes a valuable corporate asset indeed.

Dick Blodgett's experience is that "many large corporations have one or two outside writers they rely on regularly. Thus the key to long-term success in this business is to develop enduring relationships with a few corporations." Blodgett currently works with about a half dozen clients, two of which he has worked with for nearly twenty years and the others for ten years or more. "I view myself as a consultant as much as a writer," he adds, a status you can attain when you thoroughly understand the client's people, corporate objectives, and needs.

How much should you charge? Sometimes settling for too little makes sense if you feel the experience and credentials are worth it. Learn how to enhance your client's bottom line and your own bottom line will follow in step.

Focus on the goal

Most of us serve our ideals by fits and starts. The person who makes a success of living is the one who sees his goal steadily and aims for it.

Cecil B. de Mille

Remember Kipling's "six honest serving men"—Where, What, When, Why, How, and Who? In my experience as a freelance, the most important one is "why."

Analyze "why" down to its roots and the corporate book, speech, article, newsletter, brochure, or whatever cannot help but achieve the purpose for which it was written, and as a result, the client's satisfaction and the repeat business it will generate.

Why was the assignment generated? What does the client have in mind to accomplish? Who is the projected audience and what do you know about it? Why were you selected to do the job instead of one of the company's flunkeys? In a nutshell, what's the goal?

The typical corporate assignment originates with a high level executive who communicates the need to a public relations or other marketing manager who in turn spells it out for the writer. The smart and experienced communicator will explain why the project is important and what result management hopes to achieve. Sometimes this happens; sometimes it does not. The smart and experienced freelance doesn't settle for the marketing person's explanation, but makes sure his own list of questions is satisfied. Again, typically, different assignments carry different sets of objectives. Most often the underlying goal is to influence directly or indirectly the corporation's bottom line. What follows is a sampling of typical writing projects and the goals attached to them.

GHOSTED BOOK. There's big money in ghosted books, especially for big corporations. The well spelled out goal of the book I did for Willard F. (Al) Rockwell, when his relatively small company acquired North American Aviation, was to establish and solidify Rockwell's (well earned) reputation as an expert on mergers and acquisitions. Interviews were conducted, knowledge and background acquired, and the book written from start to finish with this purpose in mind.

Other ghosted book projects were undertaken with the bylined executive's personal image and career building objective in mind. Not always and not necessarily in the corporation's best interest, but it is not in the freelance's interest to look the proverbial gift horse in the mouth. This too is part of the game.

Another ghosted book I did for a corporate owner and CEO might be best defined as a vanity trip. Almost invariably books of this kind are assigned under the guise of corporate image enhancement. Sometimes this is achieved to a degree. Just as often the corporate image building effect is minimal, the underlying objective being to enhance the bylined individual's image with his or her own career growth goal. What one senior VP I have in mind wanted was a book to mail to friends, relatives, and associates, to display on the cocktail table at home, and at selected locations elsewhere. It is not the writer's place to question or judge the bottom line value or cost of such enterprises. If a CEO wants a book to boost his ego, that's his prerogative. In all likelihood he busted his gut for years to reach the point where he is able to indulge himself in this way. The writer's job if he or she is able to see through this objective is to fulfill with sensitivity and tact the role for which he was chosen.

ARTICLES—GHOSTED OR OTHERWISE. The underlying goal of virtually every corporate assignment is to sell something—either a person, a product, the organization, or an idea. How well this goal is defined, the necessary interviews conducted, and the required research undertaken, will determine the success of the venture.

COMPANY PUBLICATIONS. Corporate magazines, sometimes called in-house publications, may be confined to employees and/or widely distributed to shareholders and customers. Whatever purpose, they are the voice of the organization, and freelances who supply material for them must do so with this thought in mind. One important goal of the employee magazine is to get across the message to personnel that the company—and its top executive team—care about them, not only as employees but as human beings with human problems and human needs. A second key goal of management is to keep workers informed and up to date about the corporation's products, research and development, community service and contributions and, most important key people—leaders and decisionmakers, as well as lower level personnel whose achievements within both the organization and community are noteworthy. In short, the employee magazine is a "Hey, mom, look at me" communications vehicle. It is designed to make workers feel good about the organization, the people who run it, and the individuals they work alongside on a day to day basis. The smart freelance is self-trained to identify as a member of this fortunate group.

THE BROCHURE. Like virtually every other piece of writing, the brochure is designed to sell the company, its products, its people. No organization, for example, can be better than its people. Large corporations in particular spread the green lavishly on a regular basis in an effort to convince top achieving seniors in well rated colleges and universities that they could make no better career decision than signing on as employees. For a number of years the recruitment brochure I prepared for a Big Eight public accounting firm was one of the ripest plums in my orchard. The trick here is to understand the project not only from the client's viewpoint but from the perspective of the much-wooed seniors the brochure is intended to impress.

Similarly, client service brochures developed for management consulting firms, financial institutions, advertising agencies, and other service enterprises are intended to persuade existing and potential customers that doing business with this stellar organization is the way to go for better service, better ideas, better profits. View the project from the eyes of the customer and you've got it made.

More spooky stuff

What's more important to you, glory or money? No question that seeing your name as the bylined author of a feature story on the cover of a magazine, or even more so on a book, is a great ego boosting experience. Corporate writing usually denies you this pleasure. Some freelances turn up their noses at ghostwriting as an example for this reason.

This never bothered me in the slightest for two reasons. I'll admit, I'm as ego driven as the typical freelance writer. But, for one thing, the way I've been treated by corporate clients provides me with ego massaging to spare. For another, corporate writing isn't the only kind of writing I do. My byline and ugly face have appeared and continues to appear on articles and books produced for non-corporate clients. So I can strut my stuff to neighbors and friends I want to impress to my heart's content.

But there's another factor that to me is even more important. Call it the Self-indulgence Alternative.

I have spoken to I don't know how many freelances who grouse, however financially successful and independent, that they are dissatisfied with both their lives and careers. "How so?" I asked one writer who specializes in food preparation and in health related subjects who earns a comfortable living.

"I don't know," she frowned. "What does it all add up to?"

"What does what add up to?"

"I don't know. This day after day routine. Okay, I think I do a good job. My editors are happy. I'm well compensated. But it's the same thing over and over. I keep telling myself that one of these days I'm going to tackle something important, something meaningful; I have a novel in mind, and a book on politics that would be a crapshoot at best."

"So why don't you?" I asked.

"Sure, easy to say. But I don't have the guts to sacrifice the sure and steady income from this stuff that I write."

Have such thoughts ever assailed you? They have me, and I don't know how many other freelances. My answer is and has been for decades corporate work. I am not wealthy. I earn a comfortable, perhaps a shade more than comfortable, living. My savings and investments, I expect, will keep my family secure for the rest of my life. For this—my financial independence—I have corporate writing to thank, more than any other single factor. You know what I'm talking about. My comfortable income from corporate work provides the leeway I need to indulge myself in projects that I—rightly or wrongly—regard as "meaningful and important."

Lord knows I crowed enough about my achievements and triumphs in this book. So it's time to dwell for a moment (not too long) on my flops.

Like many nonfiction writers I have been obsessed, and continue to be obsessed, with a burning desire to write a significant novel. The lure to do so can be strong. To date I have written three novels. One took me three months to do. The $1,000 advance was all the money I ever saw from it, and I have never been able to find the paperback on a shelf—anywhere. That's my successful novel. The other two—one I still consider the best writing I've ever done—bombed. One literary agent gave it a whirl with some flattering comments but no takers. I lost count of the number of publishers I sent the book to subsequently.

On top of that, there's the vacation and recreation consideration. I am in the enviable situation that the wife and I can take off for a week or so any time the spirit move. I am also something of a duplicate bridge addict and devote an afternoon a week to this pastime. In addition, I play sax and clarinet in a Big Band, combo, and concert band. One afternoon a week is set aside for rehearsals.

My kids are now grown up and on their own. But in years past, with a family to raise, and at one point two homes to support, how could I afford such indulgences? You guessed it. The key was corporate writing. The Self Indulgence Alternative. The good steady income from corporate work permitted me to invest a portion of my time, not only on that "important and meaningful" stuff, but on fun and games as well. The Great American Novel will probably never materialize. So what? I tried. As a blue-eyed crooner once put it: "I did it my way."

How smart do you have to be?

Morons need not apply, but you don't have to be brilliant, not even very intelligent, to be a successful freelance writer. What you do have to be is ambitious, persistent, very responsible, and with the ability to bounce back from setbacks. In my early experience I could have papered the Taj Mahal with the rejection slips I received.

On top of that, you have to be the kind of person who is willing to work hard, and who doesn't wax paranoiac as a result of working alone. Fortunately, I never had that problem. As a supervisor and manager I was responsible for the performance of too many mediocre and don't-give-a-damn people. I hated that aspect of my job. As a freelance, I'm responsible for my own performance alone. If I do well, I succeed. If I flounder or goof off, I fail. I like to think that's the way it should be.

Admittedly, cabin fever, working alone for days on end, constitutes a problem for some writers. It did for my talented daughter, Madeleine Payamps. With a small child to raise, she wanted to be at home to do the raising. Having worked as a writer for Bristol Myers and other large corporations, she had become a master at her trade. When she went freelance full-time, she was able to clinch a number of well paying Fortune 500 accounts. But long accustomed to working with people, cabin fever did her in. So was her corporate writing experience a waste? Not a bit. With her experience and background she landed a writing job with a top-rated consulting firm. Her income today exceeds anything her old man ever made. So however you view it, corporate writing, done right, almost always pays off.

Corporate assignments constantly put me in touch with people all over the country. Has cabin fever ever plagued me? Not remotely. For one thing, my work constantly put me in touch with people all over the country, either in person or by phone.

Working alone for a week or two at a stretch never bothered me. If it had I would have had no problem landing a well paying corporate job.

From a corporate writing standpoint, what you don't know you can learn, and in the learning process you will get plenty of help from the people who hire you. Corporations these days, large or small, need vast storehouses of information to function profitably. Client have as much of a stake in your successful performance as you do. They are thus ready and willing to open knowledge and research pipelines to freelance writers who serve them. In my experience, too often the problem is too much information,—the challenge, to distill out the most pertinent—instead of too little. The tough job of organizing your work and learning your trade doesn't require brilliance; it requires setting the tired old nose to the grindstone.

Tips from the paymaster

What must a freelance writer who wishes to submit ideas and proposals to corporate publications know? Who better qualified to answer this question than the person on the receiving end of the queries? I asked the question of Sandra Grant Carcione, Senior Editor, Marketing Communications for CAN. She was kind enough to oblige. What follows is her counsel for freelance writers.

- Send clips of relevant articles and note industry experience in your cover letter. If you're targeting a magazine, send feature articles not short news pieces. I like to know that a writer can organize material from various sources.
- Be persistent, but not obnoxious. I frequently receive materials from freelances, but they often get pushed aside "until I have time." However, I make sure to read the clips, bios, etc. of writers who follow up by phone.
- Be willing to take guidance from the editor. I send writers an assignment letter that outlines the slant I want writers to take. Why? It prevents rewriting and substantial aggravation later. (I conduct pre-article research and speak to high level sources *before* I give out the assignment.) Too often, I've found when I've received the first draft that the writer ignored the assignment letter.

- Ask the editor for sources. It will ensure that the writer is talking to the right people.
- Be willing to spend the time the article requires. I recently had a writer grouse because "the article tried to cover too many products." The article was about all the products a specific department offers. The real problem? The writer did not want to spend the time needed to do the article correctly. Editors aren't stupid; we know when a writer has turned in a sloppy job.
- Request and read background information about the topic. I get calls from sources who are annoyed with writers who ask basic questions.
- Meet deadlines. When I give a writer three to four weeks to write a 2,000 word piece, it is annoying to hear "I couldn't reach the sources," after the first draft is already three days late. Writers need to contact sources early on. Then if they cannot connect, call the editor immediately. He or she can usually intervene or provide alternate sources.

FOUR

The rules of the selling game

We are all salespeople every day of our lives. We are selling our ideas, our plans, our enthusiasms to those with whom we come in contact.

Charles Schwab

How can a freelance tell when he or she is financially independent and secure?

This question was posed to financially independent and secure freelance Judy Wade of Phoenix, Arizona. Here is her reply:

- The first symbol of financial security is being able to quit your day job. When you can pay the rent, and all attendant bills, by freelancing, you've achieved a measure of financial security.
- Somewhere in your career you realize you're not having to query as often. Editors come to you with repeat assignments, and sometimes even editors you've never met call with assignments, based on seeing your byline and liking your work. That makes you feel pretty secure.
- When you hit some self-set financial goal...say $50,000 per year...and sustain it, you realize financial security is yours.
- Finally, when losing a hoped-for assignment, when a dry spell hits, when a magazine goes belly-up while still owing you a substantial chunk of change, and you *still* can pay the bills and take a vacation, you know you're financially secure.

In short, when you are free, not only from pressing financial obligations but from anxiety and the night terrors as well.

Thank you, Judy. Makes sense. But what does it take to achieve this enviable status? Among other things, it takes knowing how to sell and then putting what you know into practice.

Face it: If your goal is to be a successful freelance writer, like it or not, you will have to be a successful salesperson as well. I say "like it or not," because some writers I know don't like it. They reason, my skill and talent is writing. I can't afford to sacrifice writing time to other pursuits like selling. The harsh reality is: You may get by with this philosophy, but you won't get rich. To get rich, you have to hustle. You have to cover your territory and compete.

Like any other sales rep, as a freelance you have two principle "products" to sell: *yourself*, and *The "Line of Goods" you market.* Each is equally important.

Whether the product is carpet tacks, fish hooks, or feature articles, prospects are out to get the best quality they can at the lowest possible price. If they achieve this goal, their own jobs will be secure, and they will keep coming back for more, which is specifically what you are after. The problem that stands in your way and in the prospect's way can be defined with a four-letter bugaboo.

Risk

Just as you would be afraid to spend days working on an article if you were uncertain about the editor's intentions or the publication's survival and ability to pay, the editor is afraid to invest time and money in an author who may or may not do an acceptable job. So your sales goal as a freelance is to convince prospects they have nothing to worry about. How do you do that?

"By producing terrific prose that sings and inspires," you might reply. But unfortunately this isn't the answer because the performance convincer occurs after the fact. You have to get into the barn before milking the cows. The editor unfamiliar with your ability on a first hand basis can't afford to take the chance that the assigned feature might turn out okay. He or she has to be sure, or as close to sure as possible, before rolling the dice.

Repeat business—the key to selling success

Repeat business and multiple mileage. Clinton, New York, freelance Jack Behrens cites his "acquired plan for reusing salable ideas" as a key factor in the financial security he has achieved over the years.

Opening a new account doesn't necessarily make a sales rep a pro; getting repeat business sparked by multiple mileage does. The analogy for freelance writers is clear. You sell an article or a book, good for you. Even better for you is the reuse profit you cash in on from your time investment in the research made in doing the project. This applies doubly if the project in question is a book.

Too many writers write too many books that are one-shot affairs. They sell the book, get it published, then go on to other things. Top freelance pros milk their published work to the possible maximum. They rework their material for different markets, devise new angles and slants, use unused material, cash in on their time investment again and again.

Within a three-year period, for example, Cedar Park, Texas, freelance writing team Paris Permenter and John Bigley sold books titled *Caribbean for Lovers, Adventure Guide to the Cayman Islands, Adventure Guide to the Leeward Islands,* and most recently, *Caribbean With Kids.* What a great way to earn a living!

A long list of books credited to Bethesda, Maryland freelance Richard Levy, a "toys and games" specialist, includes: *Inside Santa's Workshop, Investor's Desktop Companion, From Workshop to Toy Store,* and *Inventing & Patenting Source Book.*

Get the picture? The simple formula: Specialization + Repetition and Reuse = Financial Security.

It's easy once you get the knack. Find a subject that will sell and sell again and, like the sales rep who keeps getting repeat business on the office equipment, floor covering, or glassware he peddles, your continuing income—and outcome—will be assured.

Knowledge attained is an asset that can stay with you all of your life. What has this to do with repeat business? A great deal. Since graduating high school or college, what working experience have you had? Talk with a dozen writers and you will be able to compile a long list of stints ranging from actor to zoologist. One of my own many ventures was employment by a security consultant who specialized in uncovering corporate theft and dishonesty. A dead-end PR job for a cheap employer, I quit after six months. But the knowhow I obtained was invaluable. Subsequently, as a freelance, I cashed in on what I had learned again and again.

My first cash-in attempt consisted of article queries to business and management magazines. Response consisted of some editorial interest accompanied by $50 fee offerings, a loss proposition. Little wonder. From the editor's point of view, why pay important money for good material you can get for free? Since press exposure constitutes bread-and-butter, and sometimes gravy, for consulting firms, they hire their own people in an effort to get their message across to the business community. When articles are submitted it is on a freebee basis, since the goal is not the writing income but the coverage. As a result, most editors display little if any interest in freelance solicitations that would require them to shell out money.

Still, since my information was valuable I gave birth to a brainstorm. I contacted a former English teacher named Saul D. Astor, who owned a consulting firm called Management Safeguards, and proposed a deal: My writing service on a contingency basis. Articles written by me and bylined by him. If I placed an article, I would bill him for my time at a specified dollar amount per hour with from-and-to parameters set. If I failed to place the piece, it would cost him nothing. Saul, who became a good friend, was thrilled with the proposition. Several articles were placed in management, hospital, retail, and other publications with all parties to the deal making out.

In my experience as a business writer, I learned early on that there are certain messages corporate management needs to drum into the heads of its people repeatedly. For more than 20 years I wrote *What an Executive Should Know*, *What a Supervisor Should Know*, and *What a Salesperson Should Know* booklets for The Dartnell Corporation, an average of 20 or more per year on subjects ranging from customer service and teamwork to communications and absenteeism. Applying much of the same material, I sold scores of features to The National Foremen's Institute. The money wasn't inspiring, but with virtually all the information extracted from done research, my own experience, and/or my imagination, the assignments were profitable and, most important, a reliable source of income. As a result, throughout my entire freelance writing career I have yet to experience a so-called "dry" or barren period.

Don't be anonymous

My publisher, Dennis Stovall, informed me that when he himself was a freelance writing on spec, whenever possible he contacted the editor in an effort to get him or her personally involved. They discussed such issues as slant, interviewees, sidebars, headings, and subheads—and in the process Dennis not only picked up useful guidance, but multiplied the editor's investment in the project at hand. Most important, editor and writer got to know each other on a more intimate and personal basis.

As a freelance, anonymity and financial independence are directly opposed to each other. Most successful salespeople will confirm, their best and most profitable customers are the ones they know well and with whom they are friendly on a first-name basis. It works the same way in the writing game.

It stands to reason. Editors are busy people. Still, the editor who knows you is less likely to brush you off than the one to whom you are anonymous. It's matter of common human courtesy. One of my early weaknesses as a writer was to ignore this reality of freelance life. I couldn't begin to calculate how much it must have cost me to disregard these simple and basic rules of salesmanship:

- Personalize your approach. Contact editors whom you feel might be interested in your work, then contact them again. Follow-up is important. Be persistent without being a pest, sometimes a hard line to draw. But if the editor hears your name often enough, at some point you will stop being a stranger.
- Same thing with corporate executives who are usually easier to approach and get to know than editors.
- Combine business and social intercourse when you can. Learn about prospects as human beings as well as businesspeople. Find mutual interests if you can. Attend events where you are likely to meet editors. Draw them into conversation. Send them holiday greetings, birthday cards, and acknowledgments at special events. When you contact them later by mail or telephone, call to mind your previous meeting.
- Develop referral opportunities and take advantage of them. You are a giant step closer to bridging the icicle gap if you can approach the editor with, "Harry J. Somebody-You-Know suggested that I contact you."
- Check to make sure you have contacted the right person—the one with decision-making authority. Then determine the best way to communicate, by telephone, surface mail, or email, and the best time of the day to make the contact.

Serendipity doesn't hurt either. A writer I know, like me, is hooked on duplicate bridge. One day at a New York City bridge club he became friendly with a player who just happened to be a trade magazine editor who became interested in the writer's pre-freelance legal background. "Have you ever thought of doing a column on the legal aspects of management?" he asked.

"Not really," the writer replied, "but it's a thought." Today he is into his third year of writing such a column for the trade magazine. The lesson speaks for itself: Make a friend, make a contact.

Outperform the competition from the outset

Sell your project with the editor's special needs and concerns in mind. Your goal:

> To minimize the risk factor on the one hand, and stand out from the crowd on the other. Include in your proposals not only promises of what editors who do business with you might expect, but a sampling of the actual substance involved.

The typical magazine editor is under continuous pressure to "get the book out." Book editors are no less pressured to review and evaluate the mountain of proposals they receive from day to day. As one editor put it to me recently, "There aren't enough hours in the day." Another editor said, "On ninety percent of the queries I receive I don't get past the first sentence or two."

This can work to the smart freelance's advantage. How?

1. By keeping the competition in mind when designing and developing projects for editorial consideration.
2. By framing article queries and book proposals with the editor's perspective in mind.

Take an article query as an example. You have a new slant on parenting, a can't miss brainstorm. You have carefully studied the market and selected one publication in particular where you are convinced your proposed feature will fit. You are sure that your idea, which you can describe in one short paragraph, will appeal to Donna Hardsell, the editor. But is one paragraph enough? Probably not, because it is unlikely to live up to the selling potential of the hundreds of competitive queries that will cross the editor's desk.

To outsell the competition, the trick is to do as much of the editor's work as you can. Let's suppose your brilliant idea does indeed appeal to Donna. In this case, her editorial mind's eye will focus on the finished article as it might appear in "the book." This will involve, in addition to the main body of prose, a sexy title, a provocative subhead, a strong lead, and maybe a sidebar or two. Consider how much more sell your query will have if you take the time to work out and present these four or five elements in a sexy provocative manner. Consider too that if you don't take the time for this extra work, your savvy freelance competitors most certainly will.

What applies to the article query applies doubly to book proposals, which I will deal with in detail in Chapter 8. At this point, suffice it to repeat the counsel above:

> Do as much of the editor's work as you can.

View problems as opportunities

It has been said that problems are opportunities in disguise. Want to make friends galore? Help people solve problems. Are you interested in the most fertile soil of all, corporate work? No company I ever dealt with or visited was problem-free. Executives are plagued by problems every day of their lives. The higher level the manager, the more irksome the problems. In fact, managers advance in the hierarchy based on their ability to analyze and deal with problems.

In my Chilton book, *Psychic Selling Strategies That Multiply Your Income*, I write: "Pinpoint the problem and you'll spot the opportunity." It's one of the oldest and best proved axioms of selling. Multimillionaire entrepreneur and supersalesman, W. Clement Stone, once said, "So you've got a problem? That's good. Why? Because repeated victories over your problems are the rungs on your ladder to success."

As a freelance, where do you fit into this picture? Naturally and ideally. Like the right piece slotted into a complicated jigsaw puzzle. Make every effort you can to function as a professional troubleshooter. It's easier than you might imagine. The challenge is to learn as much as possible about hang-ups and hassles plaguing companies and corporate executives you are trying to access. Become conversant with the problems. Display a personal interest, concern—and knowledge—of them. Nothing impresses an executive or editor more than coming face to face, or voice to voice, with a presumed stranger who has taken the time and effort to understand and appreciate his or her personal needs. It is clear that the freelance with first hand knowledge of a prospect's needs will be better qualified to develop ideas and strategies for dealing with them. Targeting prospect problems and being in a position to talk about them will give you a jump over competitors just as it gives sales reps in the field the advantage in trying to beat out other reps for those orders.

Analyze the market at regular intervals

Every experienced salesperson knows that last year's model, style, design, color, etc., may bomb out this year. Certain salable book and article subjects, like products and the weather, have seasons. As a freelance, timing your work to the season is of the utmost importance. I learned this the hard way. For years I had a great deal of success with career-related articles, booklets, and books. In the past year or two, I had as much success trying to sell a book idea in that genre as I might have had trying to sell a line of American flags to Slobbo Milosevic. The reason? My agent gave it to me straight. For one thing, the career market is saturated. For another, most editors won't consider a career-based proposal unless it is submitted and bylined by a celebrity. Unfortunately, I have yet to achieve celebrity status.

The variety of topics dealing with management are no longer the freelance bonanza they once were because of new realities of literary marketplace life.

1. Market saturation, which may be disregarded if the bylined author happens to be well known and a nationally recognized expert in the field. Or, equally important, a top executive for example, whose organization will commit itself to the purchase of a specified number of books. The conclusion is clear: If you have a great idea for a career book, hook up with a celebrity and you may find yourself in the running.
2. The changing economy in general, and the merger-acquisition binge in particular. Increasingly, big publishers are swallowing mediums and smalls with buying decisions being made more than ever before by the numbers crunchers. Literary merit, too often, has come to be of secondary importance.

Greed or, depending on your viewpoint, smarter and more sophisticated financial management, has taken over the executive suites in many major publishing empires, although the validity of that euphemism, is debatable. Whatever the case, book and magazine editors, pressured by bottom line-focussed bosses, carry risk avoidance to new limits these days. This may boost profits short term in some cases. But what it also accomplishes is to put a crimp in the creative efforts of many writers, freelance and otherwise, and this costs everyone more in the end. What steps can you take to keep abreast of current marketplace trends? A writer I know has become friendly with employees in large bookstores like Barnes & Noble, B. Dalton, and Borders. "Who else would be more up-to-date," he reasons, "on what's going on in the market?"

Smart thinking. This high-earning freelance keeps informed about what subjects are hot and which appear to be cooling down. Most important, he gets the latest dope from people in the best position to know.

Certain topics to be sure—sex, health, food, weight reduction, parenting, investing, etc.—always have been and always will be in demand. Which is where creative imagination comes into play. The trick here is to find provocative new angles and new ways to present the time-tested perennials and to either cash in on your own expertise or partner with proven professionals in the field.

Working your territory

Successful salesmanship is largely a matter of working your territory. Most experienced reps I've met are friendly talkative people. Opportunity seekers.

Jerry Madden, an office products salesman I know, once told me, "I couldn't tell you how many sales I made in my day that originated with waitresses, service repairmen, gas station attendants, and the like."

Madden never stops prospecting and his curiosity is unquenchable. In making the rounds, if he notices a building in construction, he makes an effort to find out who will occupy it. If he sees an item in the paper reporting on a new product line, his attention immediately perks. Corporate reports of increased business often indicate an increased need for stationary products, invoices, report forms, letterheads, computer software and peripherals. Madden follows news of executive changes in the local paper, promotions, transfers, resignations. He sniffs out leads like a bloodhound on the scent. Sales pro that he is, he never stops prospecting.

Madden is also sold wholeheartedly on the team approach. As a result, he partners with as many fellow reps as he can, especially with those who carry different lines but call on the same kinds of accounts as he does.

"Just the other day," he told me once, "I got a call from a rep I know who sells a line of industrial wall decorations. He tipped me off to a customer who was expanding his plant and creating a special division to develop a new product line."

Madden got down there in a hurry, found out the name of the executive in charge of the new enterprise, wound up selling him three personal computers and an assortment of special software. He could cite innumerable instances, he says, where tips he provided for other reps bounced back to result in business for him. He likes to quote an old Chinese proverb: "One hand washes the other."

Madden's hand-washing philosophy works as well for freelance writers as it does for men and women who sell products from chocolate covered raisins to brass fittings and baby carriages. Busy writers I know run into periods when they have more business than they can handle. When an editor calls me with an assignment I'm too busy to take, as often as not I'll reply, "I'm sorry, Kate, I can't meet your time frame, but I know just the guy who can. Are you interested?" She may or may not be, but at least I try. If the job pans out, referrals won't forget it. If not, they will know I was thinking of them, and responsively, they will think of me. Of course, in making a referral, the importance of recommending a writer who is qualified to handle the assignment competently and professionally could not be overstated. That way you do two people a favor, the referred writer and the editor.

Mutual assistance arrangements pay off. The more freelances you know who are interested in exchanging referrals, assuming you have something to say and know how to say it, the more work will come your way without your having to hustle for it.

Entrepreneurial start-ups

One more time for the record: You gotta start SMALL in order to grow BIG!

When you are small and unknown, realistically, from the editor's viewpoint, you are a poor business risk. The challenge therefore is to alter your status from anonymity to someone to contend with. With this thought in mind, there are different approaches to prospecting. The common and most obvious way is to query again and again in an effort to land assignments. At the outset of one's freelance career this can be a painful, exhausting, and not very rewarding endeavor. So what's the alternative? You still have to bridge the gap between anonymity and recognition as a professional. But how?

One way, counsels Dennis Stovall, is via the regional route. "As a regional writer, through research and interviews, you will be contacting key people in business, industry, academia, politics, civic groups, associations, clubs, and other areas of society. If you have treated them fairly in your writing, you will find them to be valuable references for work. From time to time they, or their organizations, may need materials written. There is a good chance someone will think of you. For one thing they know you are already familiar with the subject. For another, they have evidence that you can research and write.

"By developing expertise in a particular subject, you also open yourself to writing jobs that you seek out. If a special interest group is large and influential, but doesn't have a publication, you may be the person to start one. If the group has a journal or newsletter, you may be just the one to write a column.

"In addition, there are many professionals with vast knowledge, a need or desire to communicate, but poor skills or simply no time to write. They may hire you for anything from editing and verifying research to rewriting or ghostwriting. If that interests you, let all your contacts know that you are available for such work. It might even help to run a notice in relevant professional publications. It never hurts to advertise."

The profitable freebee

I would never recommend this strategy. But in a recent freak situation I was told about, it worked. The freelance writer in question, scanning through a medium size magazine he had been trying for months to crack, came across an article that was in his opinion so poorly written and organized that he was struck with a brainstorm. He wrote a letter to the editor, not openly criticizing the piece, but stating, "For your interest, here's how I would have written that article." What followed was a rewrite of the feature. The contrast between the two pieces was so clear and dramatic, he believed, it would have to make the editor sit up and take notice. She did. The freelance got no response to his submission, but two months later received an assignment from the editor, the start of a long running relationship.

There's a more conventional way to gain attention and contacts whether you are a relatively new start-up or established pro. Involve yourself in a community undertaking, political or otherwise. If Candidate X gets elected let us say, you strongly believe it would be a disaster for yourself and your neighbors. The guy the community needs is Candidate Y. If this is your sincere conviction, why not get out there and write your heart out for Candidate Y.

If the School Board is proposing action you feel will be detrimental to kids in the area, don't sit still. With your persuasive ability, editorials you place in the local paper, or other publications, could just help turn the tide. If the War Against Drugs isn't as effective as it should be in your town, donate your writing skills to doing something about it. Whether you accomplish your purpose or not, you can be sure of one thing: Your efforts will be noticed and appreciated, by individuals who share your opinions in particular. And from such humble beginnings valuable contacts can be made while your social responsibilities are being fulfilled.

Ideally, your efforts towards community service in the best case scenario, should not be undertaken with personal gain as your motivation. But as experience proves, freebee efforts of this type can be a highly effective method of prospecting and calling your name to attention.

A sour note: The publisher as antagonist

One would think that if anyone would be interested in making your book or other submission a success it would be your publisher. Unfortunately, it doesn't always work that way. Horror stories in abundance have been reported by the ASJA and other writer groups by freelances who, after having written their hearts out for months—or years—on end, wind up with minimal sales and income because of bureaucratic negligence, sheer inefficiency, or indifference at the publishing end of the enterprise.

It is the responsibility of writers is to produce a conscientiously researched and written product to the best of their ability. It then becomes the publisher's responsibility to run with the product in a way that will elicit maximum interest and participation among salespeople, booksellers, and distributors. Some years back, in my own sad experience, I wrote a book for a major publisher that was extremely well received by the critical press.

My editor, in fact, confided in me that he viewed the book as a potential bestseller.

It turned out to be anything but. One reason, my editor explained apologetically, was that the firm's publicity director resigned or was fired almost simultaneously with the book's publication and release. On top of that, other books carrying celebrity bylines came out at the same time as mine. Whatever publicity efforts made by the publisher were largely confined to books bylined by the big-name authors. Promotion attempts on my book were shamefully inadequate.

It is no secret in this business that for a book to do well, it must be properly marketed. Most of the promotion—print, TV and radio interviews, etc.—were what I myself arranged. This fell far short of the bestseller requirement. Admittedly, I was at least partially at fault for failing to stay on top of the publisher's promotional effort.

Salesmanship in the literary marketplace is a two-way street traveled by both writer and publisher. You have to see to it that the work at the other end is being done.

No books in the store

One of the most frequently heard freelance laments goes something like this:

"I did the circuit religiously, TV appearances, radio interviews, the works. But what the hell was the use? The books weren't in the stores in time."

The sorry picture is clear. You're on the Today Show. The interview couldn't have gone more smoothly. The TV host is impressed by your great book, *A Surefire Way To Keep Your Kid Off Drugs*, and praises it to millions of viewers. The audience responds enthusiastically. Next day, thousands of prospective buyers flock to the bookstores around town to get your surefire secrets revealed, and bookseller after bookseller informs them that the book is yet to arrive.

Livid, you call the editor who apologizes profusely and blames the wholesaler. "Nothing like this has ever happened before," he assures you. But it has happened before and will happen again unless you take whatever steps you can to avoid it. In the meantime, the editor is unable to tell you when the mess will be straightened out.

Moral of the story for the freelance: An important part of salesmanship in this business is doing everything in your power to ensure that the publisher's salesmanship role is fulfilled. Touch base regularly with all parties involved, especially when pub date is close at hand. Make a noise. Get your editor on the horn and get him working in your behalf. If the wheels aren't turning as they should, call your agent if you have one and raise hell.

Prospecting can be expensive

It can, but doesn't necessarily have to be. This refers not only to prospecting for business, but the high cost of research.

Consider research first. You receive an assignment that requires a good deal of digging for information, interviews, library trips, phone calls, whatever. Or you frame a proposal where anecdotes and facts will be needed. Remembering back to the not so good old days, I can recall how time-consuming and expensive it was to conduct such research. Toll charges, postage, time killed in writing long letters. Past tense. Today, thanks largely to toll-free calling and email, what once cost a pile of money is now accessible at little or no cost.

Same thing applies to prospecting for assignments. Many editors choose email as their preferred means of communication, messages they can reply to quickly and easily at their convenience. Corporate and editorial toll-free telephone numbers are posted on the Internet. I keep a folder of 800 numbers broken down by career and industry classifications: Various kinds of manufacturing companies, pharmaceuticals, retailers, health care, and various service organizations. Same thing for individuals: Psychologists, doctors, consultants, etc. It is a boon for freelance writers in their unending effort to keep operating costs down and their bottom line up.

Oh well, such is life. In some ways, as the world and economy shrink, the freelance's existence gets tougher and more challenging; in other ways, it is growing easier and more exciting.

FIVE

Spreading the word

Doing business without advertising is like winking at a girl in the dark.

Phil Harris

There are many ways to "advertise," and more than one way to "spread the word."

As a freelance writer, to what extent is this necessary?

More than one freelance has told me, "You are safe and secure psychologically and financially when you don't have to send out queries, when the editors come to you with assignments." One writer I know, a six-figure earner, told me he can't remember the last time he sent out a query.

Most of us aren't that lucky. What if editors aren't beating down your door; how do you attract their attention? The answer is simple. You have to get out there in the marketplace via phone, Internet, email, or on foot, and make your presence known. Someone once said, "It's not who you know, it's who knows you." Actually, it's both.

Another freelance stubbornly refuses to leave his cubbyhole. "I'm a writer," he asserts. "It's what I do; it's how I earn a living. When I don't write, I don't earn."

This writer disregards the ostrich parable. Long term solitary confinement can be as hurtful to the freelance as it is to the con who spends weeks or months in the hole. Editors can't be expected to beat down your door if they don't know the occupant or address.

A balanced life

A good argument for separating yourself from your desk from time to time is the healthy effect it can have on combating cabin fever. I don't know how many freelances suffer from this debilitating malady, but for those who do, interacting with others can be a psychological as well as economic plus.

There's no question that the best creative work you produce will be all by yourself, alone, with your mental mechanism percolating. As Thomas Edison put it, "The best thinking has been done in solitude." A Hindu proverb states, "You only grow when you are alone." No argument. But it's just one piece of the puzzle. It's hard to broaden your outlook and perspective, not to mention your contacts and connections, if you are chained to your desk so much of the time that interaction with others rarely if ever takes place.

More than a century ago, Josh Billings defined solitude as "a good place to visit but a poor place to stay."

The Tallahassee Writers Association observes on its web page that writing can be a lonely activity. "If you try to share it with your family, they tell you you're a genius or advise you to forget it and stick with your day job."

So what's a freelance to do? "The only ones who will truly understand what you are doing are your fellow writers, says TWA. So join up and move off *writer's block* into a supportive *writer's bloc* where you can polish your skills and learn from accomplished local writers, how to become a published writer." That's a solution, I subscribe to heartily.

There are other ways to *spread the word*, especially if you're not as far along in your career as you would like to be. You dream up ideas and send out queries and proposals, of course. That's one way of interacting even if largely one-sided, and you will of necessity keep on doing this until your presence and competence are well enough set to induce editors to come to you.

What else can you do? Here are some aggressive actions taken by freelances unwilling to rely upon queries alone:

- One freelance checks the help wanted ads under "Writer" regularly. Where she appears to be qualified, even though the ad is for a full-time job, she sends in a resume with an offer to mail clips. "I'm not available full-time…," her covering letter begins, "but if you need writing help in a pinch…" She doesn't recall how many ads she replied to in this way over the past year or two ("probably hundreds"), but she did receive several answers, two that resulted in work, one on a regular basis. "It was well worth the investment," she says.
- A corporate writer contacts local firms in his area. "PR and communications executives," he says, "often prefer working

with freelances who live nearby, and can show up for meetings or briefing sessions at a moment's notice." His mailing of bio sheet and clips has helped him make several contacts including one "great referral," and generated "a number of assignments," two on a continuing basis.
- Another "aggressor" checks the Local Events column of his local paper for meetings of groups where he feels interacting with people he might serve could lead to opportunities. Asked about the payoff, he frowns. "I'm not sure from a bottom line standpoint. But what I am sure of is that I need to get out of the house from time to time, and even if attendance at a meeting doesn't generate work, I sometimes pick up good ideas and information that lead to article queries and assignments."
- A part-time freelance who would like to write books full-time, told me she makes it a point to visit local booksellers periodically. "Some of the people employed there," she says, "are quite knowledgeable about what's going on in the field, especially what subjects are in demand and which are on the decline. They also have a good read on which publishers are well reputed, which more often than not get new books to the store in time, and which are the recipients of writer and agent complaints." One store manager, she says, tipped her off to a subject he felt would be in demand. The idea appealed to her and a subsequent proposal turned into a contract.
- A writer who specializes in healthcare attends medical meetings of interest. "It hasn't generated any direct assignments thus far," he says, "but I've made some terrific research contacts, and picked up some great ideas and material. Most important, it's a way to stave off cabin fever, to which I'm highly vulnerable."

The friendship ingredient

In my personal experience, one of the great things about freelancing is the friends you make. Abraham Lincoln said, "The better part of one's life consists of his friendships." Right on, Abe! Three names come to mind from out of the past:

CALVIN CLEMENTS. Clements's novels of the sea and suspense, short stories and TV scripts (*Bonanza; Have Gun, Will Travel*, and others—two nominated for Emmies) were viewed by millions worldwide. I had the good fortune to meet Cal, a former president of The Western Writers of American, more than two decades ago at a meeting of a Greenwich Village writers' club where we both became members and lifelong friends.

Knowing Cal, now deceased, was more than a social experience. One of the most talented writers I ever met, it was also a learning experience. For years we spent countless hours together, critiquing each others' manuscripts, mostly fiction, and especially dialogue. I don't know how much I contributed to Cal's savvy as a writer, but what I learned from him couldn't be measured in dollars. Years later, when he and his family moved to California so he could be near the studios, my family visited him there. We swam in his pool. When he was summoned to the studio, we took his kids to Disneyland. When we moved to Florida, Cal and his family visited us. Talk about the values of getting out of the cabin. Thank God for that Village writers group and weekly meetings that allowed me to interact with other writers.

God bless you, Cal, wherever you're writing.

RICHARD R. CONARROE. One of the best PR pros I know, Dick is the entrepreneur I went to work for part-time when I quit my "day job" to travel the freelance route. Employed by his public relations agency with offices in New York and Connecticut, he taught me more about corporate nonfiction writing than anyone—or any book—before or since.

When I went freelance full-time and stopped being an employee, I continued working for Dick as an ad hoc account executive and writer. Later we published a newsletter in partnership (Profit Improvement News) which took off for a while, but not far enough. Most important, we developed a lasting friendship which is as strong today as ever. I can't remember how many games of tennis we played, how many social get-togethers we attended, how many times we helped each other out in a spot. When business friendships are made, they work to a freelance's advantage in a countless number of ways.

HOWARD CADY. My editor at William Morrow (*Sure Fail, the Art of Mismanagement*), Howard developed into more than an advisor and "guidance counselor;" he became a very good friend. I always looked forward with anticipation to our enjoyable lunches together. He told me he respected my refusal to order an alcoholic beverage, which also caused him to defer with relief. ("So many writers feel ordering a drink is expected of them, which puts the editor on a spot.") Howard trusted me well enough to spill out his guts about the negative effects of merger mania among large firms in the publishing industry. When he bought *Sure Fail,* it was his decision alone. That's no longer the case. Today, however meritorious an editor considers a book proposal, if it's a large company, the decision to buy is made by committee, not only editorial people, but accountants and lawyers as well. Howard lamented the number of worthwhile works never published as a result.

What are the by-product benefits of friendship with an editor like Howard Cady whose editing credits include Exodus among many other bestsellers? For one thing when, after his retirement, I showed him chapters of a proposed novel, he was generous with suggestions and counsel which led me to make significant changes. Another time I got a call from him. He had gotten a query from the New York State Reality Association: "Can you suggest a writer to speak at our annual conference at the Concord Hotel in the Catskills?"

"Are you interested," Howard asked. "You can speak on any book of yours that you choose."

There was a nice fee involved, plus a weekend at the hotel for myself and my wife. I was more than interested; I was keen on the idea. So, of course, was Tess.

I selected *The Complete Book of Walking,* recently published, and brought several copies along whose sale helped fatten the kitty. We did the stint and had a ball. Such is a sampling of the values of friendship among professionals, and the unanticipated little goodies a freelance enjoys.

When does it not make sense for your fingers to leave the keys for too long? Obviously, when you are loaded with work and have imminent deadlines to fulfill. It would be dumb to tell an editor, "Sorry, I was late because I had a meeting to attend, or was canvassing prospects for work."

From time to time over the years I received calls from freelance writers offering work, most often on a referral basis, infrequently on a commission basis with the caller acting as agent. A handful of freelances have actually expanded their enterprise to the point where they have one or more "stringers" on their list. One guy I know has a "stable" of writers, freelance and otherwise, in his file. I have never gone into business for myself in this way. My personal preference is to steer fellow writers to gigs when I can; most often this tends to bounce back to my advantage later on.

Hats

A couple of decades ago I ghostwrote a book titled *The Twelve Hats of a Company President*. Like a president or CEO, as a freelance writer you are at the head of your own enterprise even if the sole employee is you. Consider how many different hats a freelance must wear to succeed.

1. WRITER—It goes without saying that the most important hat you will ever wear as a freelance is your writer's chapeau. No writer, however swamped with work and successful, can afford to sit back on his or her laurels, and stop the learning experience that results in continuing savvy and expertise.
2. COMPUTER SAVANT—I dread to think where I would be as a writer, what my income would have been, or what my currents assets might amount to, had I functioned without the help of a computer over the past two or three decades. The next chapter will be devoted fully to the miracles of the electronic age as it affects the writer. For now, suffice it to say that in my view, familiarity with the computer in general and word processor in particular, is absolutely essential to achieving financial security as a writer in this day and age.
3. NEGOTIATOR—As a freelance, however favorable your rapport with your editors, your career still boils down to a me-against-them enterprise. The old cliché, "business is business," continues to flourish anew. The publisher's goal is to get the best possible product at the lowest possible price. Your objective as a writer is to negotiate for as much as you reasonably can in accepting assignments, at least once you are in a position to do so.
4. COMMUNICATOR—Freelance writers communicate continuously as they pursue their careers. With your audience at the keyboard, with editors in clarifying assignments and negotiating the best possible deal, with research sources in obtaining interviews and gathering information, with prospects in promoting your wares. How effectively you get the message across will help determine your success as a writer.
5. SALESPERSON—The importance of your selling skills has, I hope, been adequately covered in a previous chapter.

6. MARKETING SPECIALIST—Selling constitutes only one aspect of marketing. Distribution, advertising, and promotion also count, especially if creating books is what you do for a living.
7. TV PERSONALITY—A freelance isn't expected to qualify to take over the Tonight show. But show biz skills in promoting your brain children on TV will count heavily in boosting your sales and earning power.
8. RADIO PERSONALITY—Same thing applies to radio appearances, although the strategies and techniques vary somewhat.
9. RESEARCHER—Clearly, your research skills will determine first, how useful and exciting the information you gather will be in enhancing the books and articles you write and, equally important, in how efficiently and cost-effectively you will make use of your time.

Okay, maybe not twelve hats, but I could probably come up with a few more if need be. The point makes itself. *No matter how smart or self-confident you are, you can't do it alone.* You have to get out there into the literary marketplace to pick up the many skills you will need to achieve financial independence as a freelance. In my experience there is no quicker or surer way to accomplish this than by becoming a member of a professional writing group in your area.

The interactive solution

I don't have a total count, but there are hundreds if not thousands of writing organizations nationwide. Membership dues range from small to modest, rarely high, to cover administrative and operating costs. The first group I belonged to consisted of about eighteen magazine writers who ranked from novice to fairly successful. Almost all were employed in fields unrelated to writing. Mort Horowitz, a lawyer, had sold stories to *The Saturday Evening Post* (a top-rated magazine at the time) and others. Cal Clements also hit *SEP, Colliers, Argosy,* etc., and had a novel or two to his credit. At that point I had contributed to a few pulp magazines.

We met for peanuts in the back room of a Greenwich Village beauty parlor called Patchin, and charged a pittance for dues. Members read and tore apart each others' manuscripts, established great camaraderie and had a ball doing it.

Out of the whole group, Cal and I were the only ones who became freelances. What this experience taught me more than anything else was what I was doing wrong. I also learned the immense value of interacting with other writers.

Today's writers' groups, almost exclusively nonprofit, range from tiny to heavily populated. All have a single purpose in mind: To help members learn, earn, interact, and avoid being taken advantage of to the maximum degree possible. Most of the larger better known national organizations limit new members to writers—not necessarily freelances—with a specified number of published pieces to their credits. Some are tough to gain admission to; most are relatively easy.

Today I feel privileged to be a member of the American Society of Journalists and Authors, the only writers' organization to which I currently belong. I don't know if there is another group in the country that does as much for its members—or whose members do as much for each other. But I do know this: Every well established or would-be professional writer would be well advised to become familiar with ASJA and make membership a short or long term goal.

ASJA—A summary

Listed on ASJA's web site (www.asja.org) are services that only scratch the surface of member benefits in the nation's leading organization of independent nonfiction writers with a membership of more than 1,000. The email is asja@compuserve.com.

- Monthly newsletter, with inside information on the writing industry.
- Exclusive referral service for both full-time jobs and client assignments.
- Seminars and workshops.
- Private section on JFORUM, the Journalism Forum on CompuServe, where members meet daily to share information about the writing business.
- Extensive professional resource lists to facilitate networking, covering everything from agents to office equipment.
- Discount services.
- Authors Registry membership, facilitating royalty payments for database and electronic rights.

Eligibility

To qualify for membership an applicant must have credits for a minimum of six articles published in national periodicals or major regional magazines or newspapers; or two nonfiction books, or one book and a contract for a second.

Joining ASJA is not cheap. As of 1999, if accepted to membership, a $25 application fee was applied to a onetime initiation fee of $100, $165 annual dues—but if freelancing is your career, it could be the best investment you ever made.

The ASJA Newsletter

If this monthly publication was all you received as a member, your membership would still be worth the price. Several columns and features provide expert answers to writer-related questions and problems, legal and otherwise. A "Warning" section tips you off to publications to avoid as a result of excessive complaints with regard to failed or long delayed payments. "Market Monitor" briefs you on editorial changes and who wants what in the literary marketplace. A "Pay Check" roundup clues you in to how much has been paid and by whom during the previous month for articles, books, and miscellaneous assignments.

Writer's referral service

ASJA's referral service, formerly Dial-A-Writer, encourages corporations, publishers, public relations firms, and individuals to contact ASJA when professional writing assistance is needed. Lists of writing opportunities are published regularly, and members are encouraged to investigate projects that appeal to them. Over the years my income from ASJA-generated assignments exceeded my annual dues many times over.

An annual Directory of ASJA Writers with individual listings for each member spells out specialties, expertise, publishing credits, agents, and awards. No self-respecting PR firm or department would be without one.

Web sites

ASJA member Web sites are as varied as the organization's individual members. Included as part of ASJA's "home page," sites typically provide bio information, writing samples, book descriptions, and whatever other information a member might feel is useful with a spread-the-word objective in mind. As you will see in Chapter 6, some freelances earn significant dollars from the hits made on their web sites.

Will it pay for you to join a writers group? As these pages make clear, freelances run into all kinds of problems relating to rates, payment, rights, contract terms, and much more. All writers organizations have their members' best interests in mind, and have the ways and means to right wrongs. "Don't get mad," goes the Kennedy family's longtime political credo—"get even." With a professional writers group lined up in you behalf, you don't have to sit still for editorial abuse or any other kind.

Not the only kid on the block

Okay, you're not eligible at this point in your career for ASJA membership. You don't want to shell out the cash. Or, for some other mysterious reason, you decide ASJA isn't for you. That's your privilege. But it doesn't mean you can't, or shouldn't, take advantage of one or more of the hundreds if not thousands of other writing clubs that flourish in all fifty states. Several ASJA members, if fact, belong to more than one group, most commonly regional organizations and clubs that specialize in various aspects of writing.

What, specifically, interests you, or occupies much of your time? No matter how narrow your specialization—Romance, Family Relationships, Parenting, Business, Education, Boating, Aviation, Cars, Nutrition, Food, Music, Military, Outdoors, Travel, Whatever—the odds are good there's a writer's group where you can profit from interaction with its members. Chances are also high that wherever you live, you will find a group within reasonable access of your home. A great many have web sites on the Internet. Costs vary, often depending on various membership categories. Most often these are cited on the organization's web page. Many groups include editors, agents, photographers, illustrators and other professionals—and/or semiprofessionals—on their rosters in addition to writers. A great many publish newsletters with information of specific interest to members. Several groups have chapters throughout the U.S. and worldwide.

Here, excerpted from the Internet, is a small sampling to help whet your appetite:

- THE NORTH AMERICAN GUILD OF BEER WRITERS (www.beerwriters.org.writer) "was established in 1994 to champion informed coverage of beer in all its aspects and to help beer writers grow professionally." (How specialized can you get?) The organization's goal is to "encourage writing that is informed, accurate and fair-minded" on any and all aspects relating to beer. Annual dues are $50.

- THE SOCIETY OF CHILDREN'S BOOK WRITERS & ILLUSTRATORS (www.scbwi.org) "is the only professional organization dedicated to serving the people who write, illustrate, or share a vital interest in children's literature. Whether you are a professional writer, a famous illustrator, a beginner with a good idea, or somewhere in-between, SCBWI is here to serve you." Dues are $50 a year for associate memberships.
- FLORIDA OUTDOOR WRITERS ASSOCIATION (www.fowa.org). Chartered in 1946, "through the years FOWA has evolved from a small group of fishing and hunting enthusiasts to a large group of dedicated professional outdoor communicators." The stress is on professionalism. For approval, new candidates must have a specified minimum number of paid magazine or newspaper articles to their credit, and must be sponsored by an existing member. Dues, with some variations, are $85 per year.
- THE MYSTERY WRITERS OF AMERICA (www.mysterynet.com/mwa) "is the leading association for professional mystery writers. Members of MWA include most of the major published mystery writers, as well as screenwriters, dramatists, new-media writers, editors, publishers, and other professionals in the mystery field." There are four categories of membership: Active, Associate, Affiliate, Corresponding. Annual dues vary from $32.50 to $65. There is no initiation fee.
- THE AMERICAN MEDICAL WRITERS ASSOCIATION (www.amwancal.org) "is the leading international professional organization for biomedical communicators. Founded more than 50 years ago, AMWA provides medical writers and editors with opportunities for professional development in a social and supportive atmosphere. Members willingly share their knowledge and experience with others interested in a career in medical communications." Open to anyone in the medical field, dues are $95 a year.

- THE AMERICAN CRIME WRITERS LEAGUE (www.klew.com/acwl.html), "was founded in the late 1980s by a group of writers who wanted a private forum for exchanging ideas, complaining about almost everything, and trying to understand this decidedly wacky business..." If you earn money the hard way, ACWL adds, we want you. Annual dues are $35. The group's web site quotes Olin Miller, who says, "Writing is the hardest way of earning a living, with the possible exception of wrestling alligators." Maybe so, but it's the most fun way as well.
- WYOMING WRITERS, INC. (www.wyowriters.org) "is focused on helping Wyoming writers achieve their full potential. Organized in 1974, the organization has helped a full generation of writers develop expertise, receive recognition, and find their true voice in the American West." The membership consists of 188 writers from 16 states. Dues are $25 per year.
- BOULDER WRITERS ALLIANCE (www.bwa.org/brochure/index.htm) BWA in Boulder, Colorado, is "open to all kinds of communicators—technical writing and editing, copywriting, marketing communications, journalism, fiction and nonfiction, online help, World Wide Web design, desktop publishing, graphic arts, and more." In short, you name it. BWA's member *Directory* lists the names and skills of all members, and is widely distributed throughout the Boulder area. Job and assignment leads are for members only. Annual dues are $25.
- SAN DIEGO WRITERS' COOPERATIVE (www.sandiegowriters.org), not surprisingly, stresses the cooperative aspect of writers working together to benefit themselves, the organization, and the community. "We promote writing classes, seminars, readings, and related events to support both beginning and established writers, and everyone with a love for the written word." Community Outreach meetings are scheduled on a regular basis.
- HEARTLAND WRITERS GUILD (www.webcurrent.com/Heartland_Writers) quotes Robert Vaughan as Ernest Hemingway: "In writing as in all else, the quest is the thing. You are never more alive than when you struggle to create life from words..." Monthly meetings feature speakers and topics of in-

terest. An Expressions message board has been designed where "a virtual community for writers is taking shape, as well as a new email discussion list."
- THE NATIONAL ASSOCIATION OF SCIENCE WRITERS (www.nasw.org/brochure.htm) was established in 1934 by a dozen pioneering science reporters at a meeting in New York. The purpose was to create "a forum in which to join forces to improve their craft and encourage conditions that promote good science writing." NASW "is a must for science writers who want a fast, incisive airing of the issues and controversies of our business." A global organization, annual dues range from $15 for students to $70 for regular foreign members."

To repeat, the above is no more than a sampling. An untold number of clubs, unlisted and unpublicized, meet regularly in regional locations throughout the U.S. and Canada. Regardless of the stage of one's career, from novice to well established professional, there is a just-right organization for anyone and everyone who is launched or aspires to be launched on a writing career.

Many members of national writers organizations such as ASJA, The Authors Guild, National Writers Union, etc. belong to one or two other writers groups as well.

It makes sense, particularly if you are highly specialized such as medical writers, to join a second organization with your specialty in mind.

ASJA's Cathy Dold specializes heavily in environmental and health writing. She belongs to both The Society of Environmental Journalists and The National Association of Science Writers. "These two organizations," she says, "focus on the topical side of writing as opposed to the business side of freelancing." Dues are much less—$35 for SEJ and $60 for NASW. But "I do get a lot out of them," she adds. "Contacts with other science writers, assignment referrals, name recognition among colleagues and hence work down the line, keeping up with science and enviro issues, etc. I've also made many friends from all the groups—especially among the freelances who are so happy to find kindred souls." (Aside: Don't sell the psychological factor short.)

What's in it for me?

Writers groups are formed with specific goals in mind designed to help members work more enjoyably, earn more money, improve their craft and pride in professionalism, and avoid being taken advantage of. What follows is a rundown of the benefits of membership available to writers—freelance and otherwise, beginners or pros—whatever their level or special interest might be.

MEETINGS—attended by editors, agents, and fellow writers. Guest speakers, often editors, discuss their needs and requirements. This is your chance to interact with other writers and cry on their shoulders if so inclined. You can meet editors, use them as sounding boards for ideas, get to be a name with which they're familiar.

NEWSLETTER—keeps you up-to-date with what's new in the industry, announces seminars, courses, events. Clues you in on publishers' personnel switches, resignations and firings. Lists news of members' published material, media appearances, and awards. Serves as a forum for members to air their views and suggestions. And much, much more.

DIRECTORY—annual list of members includes capsulized individual bios with credits, credentials, awards, and areas of expertise. Distributed to employers and professionals in the field.

LEADS—assignments and job referral services.

RESOURCES—access to information ranging from data about members and typists, publicists and others who serve them, to publishers, agents, and packagers.

WEB—Organization's home page on the Internet including member web sites touting their expertise, achievements, and service offerings.

COMPLAINTS—member services designed to address and redress editorial and other injustices.

CONTRACT—specialists who analyze editorial contracts in an effort to keep you from being shortchanged by publishers, and helping you to understand the various clauses without the need for a law degree.

INSURANCE—many writers organizations offer affordable group insurance policies, often with significant savings.

RATES—shared information network provides the specifics on what book and magazine publishers currently pay authors for their labors.

EDUCATION—information about writing classes, seminars, writers' hideaways, etc.

DISCOUNTS—on a variety of products from event attendance and classes to publications, travel, lodging, and more.

AWARDS—who was honored for what, and why.

Beyond membership

Every organization of any kind that I have ever seen or participated in consisted of two categories of members:

1. The handful who sacrifice, work their butts off, give generously of their time and their efforts, and
2. The rest of the group who do little more than cash in on the group's services and benefits.

American Society of Journalists and Authors' Dodi Schultz, former president, vice president, chair of the publications committee, and member of numerous other committees—all voluntary and unpaid—more than qualifies for the number one classification above. A busy, prolific, and highly successful freelance of books and articles on medical and other subjects, why does she do it? Converting her investment of time into earnings potential from writing, her contribution would clearly net down to thousands of dollars.

So although Dodi's giving obviously outweighs her getting, is her service as an official of ASJA exclusively pro bono work? Not at all

She says, "The area in which I've mainly been active, publications in general and the newsletter in particular, required me to follow news in the publishing industry. This has given me far greater knowledge and grasp of developments in that industry than I'd otherwise have, unquestionably an asset.

"That activity, among others have made for a certain prominence in the group; most members are aware of my name. Some activities more than others result in interaction with other members. Any officership or governing body participation does that. Thus, I'm known to several members both personally and by repute. Has this led to paying gigs? Absolutely! Nor does it indicate that I'm better or more skilled than someone else. It simply comes down to this: When a question of an assignment or paying project comes up, and recommendations are called for, people will suggest "those colleagues who come readily to mind."

The ancient advertising principle of name recognition. It's as simple as that. Dodi adds, "Obviously, you must be competent at what you do; people won't risk their reputation by recommending anyone known or suspected of being unskilled or unreliable. But if you are active in your organization, your name will come to mind."

Dodi goes on to say, "Let's not restrict participation to "official capacity." Anyone can become involved in an organization's activities." ASJA's Directory lists 16 standing committees in addition to special projects and events. In your own organization, check what interests you. Review what you are good at and how you can best contribute. Ponder what the group is doing now, and what it could, should, or might be doing. Ideas are the starting points of progress. Writers organizations are, or should be, cooperative groups. What you think and how you feel are important. And, as experience proves, involvement helps spread the word.

SIX
Cashing in on your computer

Writing without a computer is like rowing a boat without oars.

Ray Dreyfack

NOTE ONE: You may skim or bypass this chapter if you are a sophisticated computer, email, or Internet user.

NOTE TWO: This chapter makes no attempt to offer technical advice about the computer. I am not qualified for that.

My conservative estimate is that over the past two decades the computer has more than doubled my productivity. Equally important, it has taken 90 percent of the drudgery and tedium out of my work and has injected a vital fun element into my labors. Thank you, Microsoft, AOL, et al. My computer is more than a tool; it is, to understate the case, my (usually) dependable right arm.

Freelance writing is a time-intensive occupation. The typical employee, corporate or otherwise, gets paid regardless of how many hours he kills or wastes on the job. As a freelance seeking to achieve financial independence, you drive a different buggy. Your earnings depend largely on the number of hours you devote to your profession. The computer's chief function is to optimize your time commitment in a variety of ways.

Here are the five main uses to which I put my computer:

1. Composing
2. Editing
3. Research
4. Email
5. Proposals

Composing

History's great writers, from Shakespeare and Tolstoy to Edith Wharton and James Joyce, are revered for their contributions to literature. But I've seen little credit accorded for the countless long-suffering hours these masters endured transferring their words of wisdom to paper. My God! Even if I were capable of creating such masterpieces as *War and Peace* or *Ulysses,* I doubt I would have the patience and stamina to transcribe my thoughts via a quill pen or even a typewriter keyboard.

Recalling my early, pre-computer days, pounding away on the old Underwood, I ponder with dread the laborious time-consuming task of editing and revision, redoing and retyping two, three, and even four drafts of a manuscript before judging it editorially acceptable. Editorially acceptable, but not necessarily grammatically correct and free of spelling errors.

Them days, as they say, are gone forever. Using a word processor (MS Word), I key in the first draft, or a section or two of the draft. Misspelled and grammatically incorrect words and expressions are automatically highlighted, to be corrected as I type. If a word bugs me with the feeling that a better word might apply, I strike a key and come up with a rundown of alternatives. In writing an article or book chapter these days, I rarely access my thesaurus or dictionary from the shelf as I often did in the past. My computer's thesaurus and dictionary are instantly accessible, and I don't have to thumb through pages to find what I want.

Editing

Look, Ma, no revisions! As Gertrude Stein might have put it: "The draft is a draft is a draft." The nightmare of redoing and retyping is long gone. Running through the copy, I delete, change, or add words and phrases at will. Editing a manuscript on-line, for example, I conclude that the name, Algernon is pretentious and decide to replace it with George. I hit Control F on my keyboard, and presto, Find and Replace pops up. I key in Algernon alongside Find, and George alongside Replace, click All at the bottom and Voila!, all the Algernon insertions are changed to George.

Or, I decide that a paragraph in section two would fit better into section one. No problem. I place the cursor before the paragraph in question, highlight the copy, and click the cut symbol (a pair of scissors), and the paragraph is deleted. I then move the cursor to the spot in section one where I want the paragraph, click the paste symbol, and the deleted paragraph reappears. Cut and paste. Tools within tools. It's a blast. No kidding editing is suddenly fun.

Research

A major plus for freelance specialists is that they can often complete writing assignments more or less "off the top their head" with a minimum of research required. Specializing in customer service and selling, I have done articles, booklets, and book chapters, with only minimal need to access research sources outside my head. Where such assignment opportunities arise, even low paying gigs can be profitable. After all, what you sell is your time, and as often as not extensive research can eat as much of your time as the actual writing.

Your computer can chop hours—translatable into dollars—from your research requirements. I still go to the library or bookseller when I need a book. But specifically which books to access, I get from the Internet. The task is simple and speedy. My AOL service provider links me in minutes to Amazon.com or Barnes and Noble. Linking into the subject of my choice, I pinpoint and select my options. Or I click on one search engine or another—Yahoo, Hotbot, Lycos, for example. At the search box I key in my subject—anything from alligators to zucchini—and bring up a variety of sources to access. Books on the subject are suggested, or articles I can usually download.

> A critical caution, however: Despite all the good stuff on the Internet, there's a lot of dubious data and endless hype as well. Don't take what you get from the net at face value. For the sake of accuracy, double check for reliability.

Email

Writer-editor contacts

Achieving financial security as a freelance implies functioning efficiently and cost-effectively. For the author, speed is efficiency's sidekick. The faster you can get article or book queries off to the editor, the better your chance of beating out the competition, especially when hot subjects are involved. The more dependably you meet deadlines and get off the finished product to editors, the more reliance they will place on your performance, the more likely that you will be listed as a steady source in their files. Result: The more economically you will function, the better your chance of achieving your ultimate goal of financial independence.

What has email to do with all this? A great deal! More and more busy editors cite email as communication of choice. The reasons are efficiency combined with economy. While doing this book, I am alternately working on two other books. As I complete chapters, I usually email them as attachments. The procedure is simple. I establish each chapter a book as a computer file. In sending the email, I click on attachment, download the file, and attach it to the message. Within seconds it appears in the editor's computer mailbox. No printout, no paper cost, no postage, and there's no way it could reach the editor faster. And as an added incentive, email is free. (How long the miracle of free email can survive is anyone's guess.) In the bad old days, one of the thorniest problems I faced as a freelance was how to keep the telephone toll cost from eroding whatever profit I made from the assignment. Thank God, that's a concern of the past.

In sending attachments, what if the publisher uses a different word processing system from mine, Word Perfect, for example, instead of Word; Word 6.0 instead of Word 97? No problem. Before downloading the file, I automatically convert it to the system specified by the editor.

Information requests

You're writing an article with a tight deadline. You need something clarified in a hurry, or an anecdote to illustrate a point in the piece, or a statement you made confirmed by an expert, or permission obtained to use a quote. Surface mail (snail mail as it's sometimes called) can take days; phone calls can be expensive and your party may or may not be available. Your email reaches the addressee within seconds. email has become so vital and important a part of doing business today that most editors and executives check their mail boxes regularly. An important editor I deal with never wrote or phoned me. I never heard her voice; the only snail mail I ever received was a W9 form to fill out and send back. My completed assignments are sent by email only.

Editor queries

An increasing number of editors prefer author queries by email to review as they see fit. An editor I know checks her email twice daily, in the morning and after lunch. She says, "I zip through it in a hurry, respond at once to what's important, delegate secondary messages to my secretary. It consumes a fraction of the time I used to spend, which no phone or surface mail involved. Saves me roughly thirty to forty minutes a day."

Email not only gets your query to the editor instantly which adds a competitive plus, but it's the professional way for a freelance to function.

E-TIP No. 1—You want to send someone a file, for example, And you're not sure you're doing it right. Email the file to yourself as a test. If it works, you will know you're on target.

E-TIP No. 2—Warnings abound. Add this one to your repertoire. If you are doing email and receive a message from an unknown source, think twice, then once again. There are frivolous reprobates out there, and others who are downright *bad* who get their kicks poisoning computers with program and file destroying viruses.

The problem is caused when an already downloaded message either causes an attached program to execute and infect, or invites the recipient to open such a file. Now that so much email software simply downloads mail wholesale, the key—just like Ma said—is not to open suspicious packages.

FreEmail

There are any number of ways and places you can link up to get email for free. For example, an Internet search as I am doing this chapter lists Microsoft's Hotmail, AmExMail, Juno, Doghouse Mail, and Fiberia, as well as sites offered by such service engines as AOL, Yahoo, Bell South, Lycos, and Hotbot. This is just a small sampling. Free email service links your computer to a local access number which means you hook up to it free of charge. Lacking a local number, long distance charges would apply.

In South Florida where I live, the public library network has established a free email resource called SEFLIN (for Southeast Florida Network), especially useful for writers seeking books and articles available through the library system. SEFLIN also allows subscribers to access the Internet.

Service engines like Yahoo, Lycos, and Hotbot, along with providers like America On Line and Bell South, offer free email as a competitive tool. Microsoft, for example, came up with Hotmail, in response to AOL's vast subscriber list. Most email offers are laced with pros and cons. Bell South, for example, makes access to 800 toll-free subscriber lists easy and fast whereas, as of this writing at least, AOL provides only limited access. As we shall see in a minute, this can be of critical importance to the freelance writer seeking to achieve financial independence.

A major disadvantage of many independent free email providers is that subscribers must wade through and delete a slew of advertising glop before they can access what they need. I know at least one writer who signed off freebee system for this reason and switched to a provider such as AOL or Compuserve where tons of ads didn't bug him.

That priceless 800 tool

For me as a freelance, "800" (alias 888) are magic numbers that helped lead to financial independence. A great many, if not most, medium and large size organizations can be reached through toll free numbers. In my source file I keep lists of profit and nonprofit organizations broken down into categories of particular interest to me as a freelance. Public relations firms, for example, are excellent idea sources. Their goals and mine coincide. Ditto for management consultants, psychologists, and many manufacturing, and publishing companies, publicity being a prime key to business inquiries and name recognition. In writing my bestselling mail order book on customer service, for example, calls to PR departments of dozens of companies from Digital Equipment and IBM to Otis Elevator and Xerox yielded information, suggestions, and quotes that helped make the content unique.

I couldn't begin to estimate how much time and money toll free numbers have saved me. This held especially true in the bad old days when I had no choice but to accept low-paying assignments. The difference between accessing information and quotes by means of toll free calls, as opposed to long distance calls, often made gigs profitable that would otherwise have wound up as no-win engagements.

Lists of toll free numbers are available in most local libraries. But bringing them up via the Internet is often faster and eliminates travel time.

Proposals

With rare exceptions, the days when a freelance could mail an editor a sample chapter of a proposed book with a rough outline and covering letter, and anticipate a responding letter or phone call of acceptance, are long since gone. Most often today, the proposal that sells consists of several pages, is complex, time-consuming and, with the exception of very small publishers, must undergo approval by a committee of editorial, sales, legal, publicity, and financial executives. The corporate objective: To take as much gamble as possible out of the risky business of book publishing.

We'll get into the elements of a successful book proposal in some depth in the next chapter. But for now, suffice it to say, that the computer's role in making a book proposal sexy and salable is every bit as important as it is in the writing and editing of its chapter by chapter content.

What it takes to be safe and secure
You will need a guru

I have been wrestling with computers and, before that, word processors—after abandoning my trusty (now rusty) old Underwood—for roughly a couple of decades, and I'm not ashamed to admit I still consider myself a computer ignoramus. As remarkable and powerful as the pesky contraption is, from time to time strange things happen. The machine hangs up. Weird error messages appear, and mysterious cautions that can be downright intimidating. Suddenly your work disappears from the monitor. You're hip deep in a program and you can't get out of it. You're unable to turn off the machine in the proper and recommended way. A critical file is mysteriously lost.

In my experience, when electronic crisis strikes and seems to make an imminent deadline impossible to meet, just two alternatives exist.

1. Panic.
2. Call a guru.

I learned long ago to opt for the guru. Gurus are nerds who have made the computer their life's work, just as you have made freelance writing yours. My guy charges $20 an hour for his time. His response to my SOS calls rarely runs over an hour. One of the super bargains of the century.

Don't let this scare you off. According to my records, I had to call my guru three times over the past year. Once, he put in an hour-and-a-half to squash the pesky bug that was interrupting my work. Twice, his time charge amounted to less than an hour. He's almost always nearby so that travel time isn't a factor. Once, when I was really in a bind, his response time was two hours. Another time, he showed up the next morning. A third time, he was on vacation and a substitute guru filled in for him. Like when your doctor is unavailable, an associate is on call. Most often, I phone or email my guru for a suggestion on how to do this or that for which he doesn't charge me. Embarrassed, I usually pad his bill to the next hourly mark. He's embarrassed to take it.

Possibly because I'm a mechanical moron, I view my guru as a security blanket, and I keep his number handy. I also know that even should I live to be 206 I will still be a dummy so far as the computer is concerned and that my guru is indispensable. More on this later.

What if your computer crashes?

I've been lucky; it's never happened to me. But I've heard stories. Computer hard drives have been known to crash due to inadequate surge protection in a thunderstorm, viral infusion, and other strange and mysterious reasons. I'd be hard put to think of a freelance disaster more catastrophic than the demolition of a hard drive on which critical files and programs weren't saved. It rarely happens and, with minimal care, shouldn't happen. For one thing, no computer should be installed without a surge protector to guard against crashes caused by an excess power buildup. That's simple and basic. But even simpler and more basic is the plain common sense of saving your work.

The single most important command on any computer is SAVE. It serves two functions: 1. Should a goof, undesired deletion, or whatever, cause a blowout of some kind while you are typing, the only copy lost will be the words you keyed in since the last time you hit the key command for save. It is thus of the utmost importance to save your work frequently—meaning every few minutes—while you are producing it.

It is equally important to periodically save your work to a removable disk so that even if your hard drive should crash for some pernicious reason, what you wrote will still be intact. Slip the disk into the ornery computer after it's been fixed and you're in business again. MS Word, the processor I currently use, comes equipped with a recycle bin. Thanks to this feature, when I complete and delete an article, it may be gone, but it's not forgotten. The piece gets stuffed into the recycle bin, and is thus retrievable should I need it again. Periodically, when you're absolutely certain that files in the recycle bin can be disposed of for eternity, you can delete them from the bin to avoid overstuffing.

The Internet and you

Boon or bane? Tyrant or tool? It depends on you. Most of all, in accessing the Internet, it depends on what you are using it for.

For *work* or for *play*. For the purposes of this book, I define work as freelance writing and everything that goes with it. I define play as everything else. So far as work is concerned, I rank the Internet as one of my top information and research sources.

Example: At this point, I am about to interrupt writing this section to search for information on three randomly selected subjects I might be covering as a freelance. Step one is to exit Word and my Chapter 6 document. I next sign on to America on Line.

ANTARCTICA—On AOL, I click Favorites at the top of the screen. This brings up a menu of my Favorite Places I had already designated. (On AOL, once you search and locate a site you know you will want to revisit, you can add it to your Favorite Places. Simply clicking that site will immediately get you there without having to search anew.)

For my story on Antarctica, I click on Yahoo, one of my favorite search engines, and key Antarctica into the search box that appears. Ugh! The first entry deals with Antarctica, a Brazilian beer, which I quickly bypass since my assignment involves the region, not the brew. I go on to access information about a captain's expedition, yacht cruises to Antarctica, a resort that bills itself as the gateway to the region, pictures and historical information and, through Amazon.com et al various books on the subject. That's a small sampling for starters. Other search engines will go on from there.

MULTIPLE SCLEROSIS—My next search subject is multiple sclerosis via another great search engine called HotBot. This takes me to about thirty information sites with links to other sites, plus Amazon.com and Barnes and Noble for access to books on the subject. Data ranges from general symptoms and "Doctor's guide to the Internet," "Living right to avoid MS," and sites that deal with specific disorders related to the disease. I can bring up the home page of the National Multiple Sclerosis Foundation, National

Multiple Sclerosis Society and, if I wish, can access endless sites via this and other search engines.

BADMINTON—I now click on Lycos, another button that resides in my Favorite Places menu. This brings me to Badminton's Personal Page, Australia's Sports Commission, Badminton Alberta On-Line, Badminton Association of England, Badminton British Columbia, Badminton Canada's home page, Badminton Central, "All You Need to Know About Badminton," and more. Much more if I access other search engines as well.

The point makes itself. The question is not whether you can get information you need from the Internet, but whether you will be smart and well organized enough to know when to stop.

Garbage dump

Just as clouds have silver linings, blue skies can be sullied by pollution and smog. The Internet, while on the one hand a treasure trove of valuable information, is on the other, a veritable garbage dump. Says *Newsweek* columnist Robert J. Samuelson, "The Internet has so reduced the cost of moving information that it's encouraged a lot of worthless information. Worse than that! There's enough pure unadulterated crap on the net to turn even the strongest of stomachs, and I'm not talking porno stuff alone. The world net is replete with phony and freaky come-ons and questionable data from hate groups, chiselers, endless hype, and an assortment of disreputable sources ready to help you part with your hard-earned dollars, and even your decency."

As a freelance, I access the Internet with one of two purposes in mind:

1. Research for work.
2. Searches for individuals or organizations for information about prospective purchases, health data related to personal needs, travel info, etc. For most other scans I echo the Vietnam protesters: "Hell no, I won't go!"

Don't get me wrong. There's a wealth of good stuff on the net from well reputed organizations, news and political groups. But the freelance reality of life is that browsing the net can eat time faster than termites eat wood. If your goal is to achieve financial independence as a freelance writer, it's important to differentiate between unessential information and hype, fun and games, and *work*.

Should you create your own web site?

Yes or no? It's a decision—at least for established freelance writers—to investigate thoughtfully. Some freelances unequivocally recommend setting up your own web site. Others feel it's of questionable value, time-consuming, and expensive to establish and monitor. I'm thus far uncommitted.

At this point in my career, my main interest in freelancing centers more on book writing than article gigs, although I enjoy some lucrative steadies I continue to pursue. My personal web site (see page 86) established as an ASJA link (www.asja.org) via AOL, involved no out of pocket expense and cost me no more than a few hours to set up. Its response yield has been mediocre thus far (one good assignment), but considering my investment I got the best of the bargain. Here it is. No graphics, nothing fancy.

The web site as marketing tool

Is creating a web site worth the trouble and time? It's probably worth it if you have something substantial to sell such as professional expertise that is in demand, or marketable books.

It was apparently well worth the cost to Hal Higdon, Senior Writer for *Runner's World*, whose site headed "Hal Higdon is on the Run" sold $21,000 dollars worth of books in one recent year with orders heading up. Says Hal, You need "something to lure people to your site, In my case, it's training advice for the marathon and other races. My traffic has climbed now to near 86,000 hits a week, and we can draw a direct line between hits and sales." Book fulfillment is handled by his wife, which helps Hal keep his nose to the grindstone.

It helps, of course, if you're a top-selling author like Higdon. His book, *Marathon*, does especially well on the Internet. Less successful are his non-running books such as *Falconara* and *Leopold & Loeb: The Crime of the Century*, reprint of a 1976 edition.

Talk about "achieving financial independence as a freelance writer." Higdon has refined the art of milking every buck from his writing into a science: Cashing in on reprints, collecting commissions from publishers for books sold via his site (some publishers offer 10–15%). He also collects a fee from *Runner's World* for on-site subscriptions. Makes you drool, doesn't it?

"Were I starting out as a writer today," says this top pro, "I'd be tempted to forget about writing for magazines, other than token assignments, and

BOOK PRO
THE WRITE HALF

Got a Book Idea In Mind?

Successful book publishing is a 50-50 proposition: HALF idea and goal, and no less important, HALF writing that convinces and sells.
MISSING THE WRITE HALF
YOU WILL BE ONLY HALF RIGHT!!!
My track record includes 26 books bylined and ghosted—including 3 mail order bestsellers—aided and abetted by book proposals that work! If you have a book—or book proposal—with a viable idea in mind, I may be just the guy to contact.

SUBJECT SAMPLING OF PUBLISHED BOOKS
—BYLINED AND GHOSTED—
Successful supervision * / Customer service *
Management effectiveness / Profitable salesmanship
Productivity and profits / Zero base budgeting *
Strategies of success / The corporate conscience
Successful anti-retirement / Psychic selling strategies
Career advancement…
(* indicates bestseller)

CLIENTS INCLUDE: IBM, DU PONT, CONOCO, ROCKWELL INTL., BOOZ ALLEN, CRESAP McCORMICK, CON EDISON, DELOITTE TOUCHE, HASKINS & SELLS, BANGOR PUNTA, GOLDMAN SACHS

CAN WE TALK?
(Name, address, telephone, email, etc.
Contact me by clicking here.

figure out a way to write for the Internet."

A personal web sit also helps if you are passionate about a book you are trying to sell. ASJA's Richard Stapleton's son is a lead poisoning victim. Dick's web site, which nets more hits than Irving Berlin in his hey day, is headed "Help Prevent Childhood Lead Poisoning," with a subhead that reads "Stop Lead poisoning our kids." As for Stapleton's information-packed book, "Lead Is a Silent Hazard," he uses the soft-sell approach. Clickable features on the link itself—Is My Child At Risk?, Should I Have My Child Tested?, What Can I Do?, Getting Help Locally, Links To Other Web Pages, etc.—constitutes a veritable college course on the subject.

In an article for ASJA's newsletter, Stapleton tackles the Is-a-website-worth-it? question. Quoting veterinarian author Carin Smith, he writes, "The answer is yes.'" Smith said that a software firm looking for a veterinarian tech writer linked up with her via the Internet. It's a thought to take with you. One good contact could cover all your time and expense, and then some.

Popular author Tracy Cabot is a web site enthusiast. Rated a "Top 3" Relationship site by "Beatrice's Web Guide," her home page, which gets over 1,000 hits daily, invites linkees to "Ask Dr. Tracy." Aside from promoting her "products," says Stapleton, Cabot reports that she's having a ball, that her web site is fun, and who can knock that.

Is a site hard to set up?

Only if you're a mechanical moron like me. Seriously, if your web page is simple like mine—a free link between AOL and ASJA—there's not much to it. How difficult and time-consuming depends on how sophisticated you want to make it, how much graphics you want to insert, how many links you decide to include. "Webmasters," writes *Sun-Sentinel* columnist and computer expert Laural Lorek, "would like you to believe it takes a lot of magic, technological knowhow—and time—to put a Web page on the Internet." The truth, she says, is anyone can do it.

Once you pick an Internet service provider as your host, she adds, you should select a name such as *www.laurallorek.com*, for your address. After checking to make sure the site hasn't been duplicated, you are ready for action. Unless you enjoy free linkage, Network Solutions in Hernon, Virginia. Will charge you a $70 registration fee for two years with $35 annual renewal after that. A quick probe on the Internet will lead you to several Web sites that will help you to build sites for as little as $12.99 and as much as Microsoft Front Page, which will cost you $129. Of course, more expensive and sophisticated tools are there if you need them.

A trip to your local library or bookseller will also pinpoint several current and not so current how-to books on the subject. In this case, a personal visit is preferable to an Internet probe, since an in-person evaluation of the books would be helpful.

You can also use most browsers to look at the source code (HTML) used to create the sites you like, making it easier to design your own by example.

The learning experience

From the freelance's perspective, what's the best way to accumulate computer savvy? Suggestion one—Live to 200. Suggestion two—Consider one or more of the following educational options.

First, define your needs

Innumerable—and that's an understatement—courses, books, articles, experts, groups, and marketing pros—are geared up to help make you a computer wiz. However, in my experience, an infinitesimal percentage of the total knowhow on the market should suffice for the freelance. If you must master anything at all, it would be the word processor you select. Thus, step one, before investing your hard-earned shekels, is to spell out exactly what you expect the computer to accomplish for you. Most notably, the actual writing and research.

Computer courses

Virtually every high school, college, and vocational school these days—as well as big computer stores like CompUSA—offer a variety of courses on any and all aspects of computer processing. One problem encountered with courses is that they are in most cases expensive. Another, with the need outpacing the available skilled manpower, not all instructors are as knowledgeable as they might be. Also, technological expertise doesn't necessarily imply teaching expertise. A third problem is that courses usually run several weeks or months, too long a wait between classes. A fourth is that, unless the course content is very specific (such as Quicken, for example), courses tend to be overly general. I once took a course in my local vocational school on Windows. Though reasonably priced, much of the coverage was of little or no value to me.

On the pro side, most computers courses are well organized with regard to content, and an instructor is there on hand to respond to student questions. Caution: Do not take a computer course prior to purchasing a computer. You need a machine on hand to try out and repeat what you learn; otherwise, within weeks, it will drift away like the fog over San Francisco Bay.

Books

Books are essential props for the computer user. But which books? I paid about $40 for a thousand page tome on MS Word that is virtually useless to me. I find the much shorter and better written Dummies and Idiots books easier to reference and understand.

Guru

In my own experience, I rank my guru as the primary learning resource. He does double duty as both fixer and teacher. Fixer, if I need a problem solved such as when the computer does things which (in my flawed opinion) it shouldn't be doing; or neglects to do things which (in my faulted opinion) it's supposed to be doing. At the $20 per hour cost, my guru straightens me out. Low cost and specific.

"Teacher" is the other side of the coin. Several months ago when, with my new computer, I switched from Word 3.0 to Word 97, I found my guru to be especially invaluable. He gave me a quick rundown covering the transition and geared to my particular needs in a little under two hours. Forty bucks, as opposed to hundreds in fees for most courses on the market.

This session permitted me to function as a freelance, with occasional upcroppings of problems which, for the most part, except for a phone call or two to my guru, I was able to surmount. Questions and problems that could wait I jotted down and accumulated until they totaled about fifteen. I then called my guru for another session, this time under an hour, and made a list of his answers and solutions for subsequent referral. This procedure thus far has constituted the main part of my computer learning experience.

How can so many experts afford to work for peanuts? In my area, at least, what seems to be a superfluity of computer courses are available, plus an excess of young nerds who are usually underpaid and welcome the extra work. Plus a lot of brainy young computerniks starting out as "consultants." Pick the right guy, by recommendation preferable, and you've got the bargain of the century.

Video tapes

On the con side, tapes (such as Video Professor) are very expensive—several tapes are required for complex subjects like Windows, Word, or the Internet. But in my area, at least, you can takes tapes out of the library, although owning them is clearly preferable. On the pro side, video tapes are well organized. Running them on your VCR and TV monitor, you can stop at will to take notes, and backtrack repeatedly until satisfied with your grasp of topics covered. All in all, a good learning tool.

Trial and error

Doing it, right or wrong, as most gurus would confirm, is one of the best teachers of all. In my own experience, I rank trying it out with the mouse and keyboard on a par with guru instruction. New computer users usually are afraid that experimenting with different alternatives will somehow mess up the machine. My wife is scared to death that something terrible will happen if she tries something new. There are a few very simple basic safe operating rules. Experience proves that even if these are inadvertently violated on occasion, the machine won't blow up.

Computer clubs

Misery loves company. True. So a few years back I joined a computer club in my area and attended a dozen or so meetings. On the plus side, the membership included some nice people, most non-experts like me, along with a handful of friendly sophisticated nerds who obligingly responded to questions from the inept lower class. On the negative side—too negative to sustain my membership—I found that each meeting centered on a subject (scanners, spread sheets, tax preparation, exotic new developments, etc.) of no interest to me as a freelance, and only served to consume my valuable time. I was the only writer in the group. Had there been others I think I might have hung in there.

How much of an investment?

Not much when you net it out. It's a simple matter of arithmetic. As a freelance seeking to achieve financial independence, calculate the time you would spend editing and revising your work without a computer, plus the cost of research, paper, postage, etc., and you'd be ahead of the game if you had to shell out $5,000 or more for a machine.

More good news is that given competition, technological advances, and the advertising potential of the Internet, prices have fallen and will continue to fall. My IBM clone, which includes Windows, MS Word, a host of other programs, and sufficient storage for more books than I could write in a lifetime, cost me under $1,700. A great Hewlett-Packard color printer brought the total cost to about $2,000. If you're tight on money, you can buy what you need to function as a freelance in the used computer market for a fraction of that figure.

States *Consumer Reports,* "The lowest-priced computers from big-name manufacturers like Compaq, Hewlett-Packard, and IBM have already fallen to between $599 and $950." Likely lower still, as you read this.

In my harsh opinion, if you decide a computer isn't for you, neither is a freelance writing career.

SEVEN

Should you write a book?

A good book contains more real wealth than a good bank.

Roy L. Smith

As a freelance whose goal it is to achieve financial independence, what are the pros and cons of writing a book? Or, to be precise, let's make that plural.

Cons? I can't think of any. Pros? In my career to date I have had 26 published books, bylined and ghosted, to my credit. Although book writing never has been the major source of my income, I view it as one of the main foundation stones in having achieved my goal of financial independence.

Status never hurts

Don't let this get around to editors, PR people, or publishers. But the fact that you have written a book, one book, doesn't necessarily make you an expert. It doesn't even make you a specialist. Yet. That may take another book or two, articles, other assignments, and the research that goes with it, on your specialty theme.

But—your name on the cover of a book lends you a special kind of status and, warranted or not, boosts your image a notch and opens the door to other freelance gigs. The simple rationale: Anyone who can write a book on the subject is certainly qualified to handle an article, newsletter, speech, or whatever. My customers book, for example, led to dozens of booklets and articles, and set me up as a regular contributor to newsletters on customer service and salesmanship. Fortunately, that book sold very well, usually a totally unpredictable outcome. But even if it hadn't sold well, the by-product income was substantial and eventually well exceeded the royalties. Once that book was published and publicized, the dry periods that plague so many freelances vanished like the output of a child's bubble pipe.

Continuity—the cornerstone of financial security

The transition

As a freelance, you've probably lived through this scenario. You held a job, writing or otherwise, which didn't thrill or excite you. Otherwise, you would not have so courageously sweated through a tough transition to strike out on your own.

And tough transition it is. This is no overstatement. The jump from employee to self-employed can produce the night sweats, especially if your responsibility includes supporting a family in addition to yourself. Typically, you gave up a steady job and, inadequate or not, you received a check each pay period. It was money you could, and did, count on to pay the bills for food, shelter, health care, and the rest.

Even if you hated your job, the office or plant was a place to report to each day, a "home away from home" as they say. You had a boss who told you what to do and how to do it each day. Your work was prescribed in an organized and orderly manner, 9 to 5 continuity assured.

Something to do

Why is retirement so traumatic for so many millions of people? Because all of a sudden—golf, travel, and relaxation notwithstanding—you suddenly have nothing to do. Your day-to-day routine has been blasted. It's a psychological fact of life that continuity of function is an essential ingredient of life. Being at loose ends shakes one up. For the freelance with a family, burdened by financial responsibilities, all of a sudden *not having income-producing work to keep working* can be a scary state to be in. Believe me, I know; my kids were young at the time. This in my experience through the years, more than any other factor, is what makes book writing so important to a freelance writer's psychological well being.

It's no secret to freelances that the nature of the game is to suffer both lush and dry periods. Typically, you have a number of income sources in your tickler file. You ride high for a while, elated, self-confident, completing one assignment after another, doing a good job, complimented by satisfied editors. Then pow! For no apparent reason the floodgates shut down. A couple of queries are rejected. The prospect you expected to call doesn't call. Your favorite editor who supplied you with steady work, retired, or was fired or transferred, and her replacement has her own favorite sources. So here you are, high and dry.

In the early months of my freelance career, this situation occurred from time to time. At the outset, I must confess it did funny things to my gut, nibbled away at my self-confidence. After a couple of weeks without a scheduled assignment on hand I began climbing the wall; by week three I reached the ceiling. Fortunately, at some point during this period, I signed my first book contract—with Dartnell if I recall correctly. From that time on, high and dry had lost its meaning. I never again panicked for absence of work. I had a book to work on. Something to do! In fact, I sometimes welcomed slack periods as a chance to relax and catch up on book chapters. Continuity! It's a psychological super-plus. Signing up for a book will ensure it.

There's another plus too for the hard working freelance. As an ego boosting and confidence-building hotfoot, nothing can surpass seeing one's name on a just published book. No matter how many books you have published, that feeling never diminishes.

Should you shoot for the stars?

I can think of no more seductive bait than a $75,000 or $100,000 book advance, small change for bestselling authors. Should you succumb to the lure? Absolutely!—if you are a bestselling pro, or have exclusive access to super-hot information—like, for example, Chelsea's secret engagement (a far-fetched dream at best)—that would make an editor's tongue hang out.

But if you're an ordinary grunt whose freelance goal is financial independence, facing reality makes more sense. One realty is that in recent years scores of important publishing firms have been swallowed up by the giants ruled by bottom line-focused decisionmakers. Another bleak reality is bluntly stated by author's agent Elizabeth Pomada: "One New York publisher sells 85 percent of its books to four markets: Amazon, Ingram, Borders, Barnes & Noble…If one says they don't like it, the publisher won't buy the book."

Yet another reality is that an infinitesimal number of book proposals and submissions to majors—the only ones who can afford to go astronomical on advances—wind up getting read by editors at all. Something like 99.6 percent are consigned to the "slush pile" and scanned by kids with B.A. or M.A. degrees who have less experience than the authors they evaluate. Or more likely, the manuscript is shot back unread with polite a form rejection slips enclosed—assuming return postage was submitted. Herewith an excerpt from a typical sample:

The Ballantine Publishing Group

Ballantine–Del Rey–Fawcett–Ivy–House of Collectibles–One World
A Division of Random House, Inc.

Dear Prospective Author:
We regret to inform you that, as of June 1, 1998, Del Rey Books is no longer accepting unsolicited manuscripts for publication. We did not want to take this step, and we have tried our best to avoid it... but we're simply too swamped by the constant influx of new manuscripts to be able to give any reasonable time and attention to so many submissions... (However,) Del Rey will continue to accept manuscripts that come in through reputable agents... (And so on, and on with polite encouragement included.)

What if you have an agent? More on this very soon. But for now, if you have a good book in mind, are well enough established, and possess sufficient sales savvy to interest a reputable agent—one who does not charge a reading fee—you will be assured of editorial readings. That doesn't mean your agent will sell the book. But at least you'll know it will be considered.

Hey, what are you afraid of?

Of all the liars in the world, sometimes the worst are your own fears.

Rudyard Kipling

A magazine writing freelance I know—talented, successful, prolific—pales at the thought of tackling a book. She views such a prospect as mammoth, overwhelming, unthinkable. Fuhgedabouotit!

Yet this feisty female turns out articles by the carload, despite frequent frustration at the hands of over-demanding, unreasonable, late-paying publications, some, not all. I view this pro, a specialist on a variety of subjects, as a natural to do a book. But despite attempts to persuade her, I've been unable to get through.

A good friend, why do I bug her about it? Because she's a chronic worrier. A dry period summons the frown lines to her forehead the way spring rains bring up daisies on your front lawn. Lack of continuity plagues her.

I try to convince her that writing books could help immeasurably in overcoming this problem as it has helped me in my career. Do long projects seem formidable? They shouldn't. With the right approach, books are no harder to write than articles, especially if the subject ties in with your specialization. The trick, I tell my myopic friend, is to plan, organize, outline, and think of your book as a series of chapters.

Sectionalize! This book I am writing—about 50,000 words—for example, will consist of ten chapters, the rough equivalent of ten 5,000 word articles. My magazine writer friend has produced scores of such articles. So why doesn't she take my advice? Beats me.

If you wish, you can sectionalize even further, break down each chapter by its subheadings into eight, ten, twelve or more shorter pieces.

As a freelance, the psychological value of having a book contract under your belt can't be overestimated. Typically, in signing a contract, writers commit themselves to submitting the finished product in six months to a year. In my experience, from day one of my first book contract, that put a virtual end to dry periods and the frown lines they produce. As an added plus, organizing, outlining, and sectionalizing books taught me to use this approach for any and all assignments received.

Multiply your income

"Publish or perish." You've heard the admonition from the academic community. Educational institutions compete hard for image superiority. The more status faculty members achieve, the more image enhancement the institution enjoys. At the same time, the more career Brownie points the academic accumulates, the more bucks on the pay check. Bottom line-minded freelances can cash in on this reality of campus life to the mutual advantage of themselves, their acquired professorial hosts, the publisher, and the reading public. Here's how it works.

Does your particular specialty tie in with the specialization of an academic, preferably in your area? If so, this may be an open door to an increased earnings opportunity. My customer service book is a glowing example. After contacting two marketing professors in the state, I found one who was interested in sharing my byline with him as a coauthor, and more than willing to pay me a modest sum for the privilege. Although I did 95 percent of the actual writing, the professor contributed a couple of sections, suggested a couple of ideas and reviewed the manuscript before it was submitted. A legitimate co-authorship.

The publisher was more than pleased by the added credentials the professor's name and background provided. The work itself was enhanced by his contribution so that the reader got a better book. My coauthor wound up with increased status, a negotiating chip with his employer, and a couple of consulting engagements that more than covered his financial investment. In the end, everyone involved was happy.

Should you write a novel?

Again, absolutely! Or if not a novel, at least short fiction.

Talk about "shooting for the stars"? Without question, the superstars of freelancedom are the authors of bestselling novels—guys like John Grisham, Stephen King, J.K. Rowling, Mary Higgens Clark, Tom Clancy, Danielle Steel, Nelson DeMille, Sidney Sheldon, and their ilk—all household names who need armored trucks to bring their advance and royalty checks to the bank.

Okay, I'll come down to earth. Nothing in the world—*Nothing!*—is harder to sell for the writer who is not well known than a novel. No submission is tougher to get an editor to even consider than a novel. What's more, those publishers who do review novels usually prefer to have them submitted in their entirety which I will concede is a long shot toss of the dice if their ever was one. In submitting a nonfiction book proposal, an outline and sample chapter or two normally suffices.

Why then do I unequivocally recommend fiction writing to established and aspiring authors, freelance or not? For the simple reason that, in my experience, it is one of the best investments a writer could make. Here is why.

Whether your forte is articles, speechwriting, booklets, books, or brochures, convincing dialogue is important. Articles especially are enhanced by the inclusion of anecdotes. If you have a point to make in the piece you are writing, it is often easier to make the prose more interesting and persuasive if you throw in an anecdote to color and enhance it. And as any editor would confirm, an anecdote comes alive when it is sparked by convincing dialogue.

At this point in my long writing career, I would be less than honest if I posed as a novelist. Yes, I did have one novel published several years ago (*The Image Makers*) by an obscure publishing firm that has been long since defunct. And I completed another novel some years back (*One More Time*), offbeat and off-market, that I believe contains some of the best writing I have ever done, and that I am still trying to sell. *The Image Makers* yielded a $1,000 advance which is all the money I ever saw for my six or seven weeks of work. I also sold a dozen or so short stories years ago to secondary magazines that netted an average of about $50 apiece.

So, once again, why do it? Because from the perspective of the nonfiction freelance, writing fiction is a learning experience second to none. It will stand you in good stead throughout your career—even if John Grisham, Mary Higgens Clark, or Stephen King never invites you to dinner.

Contact the *right* small press

What if you are not as yet well established and don't have an agent? My earlier counsel is well worth repeating—one more time. Think SMALL to grow BIG! *The Literary Market Place, Writer's Market,* and other reference books list hundreds of reputable small book publishers and their editorial requirements. Some offer tiny advances. Many, if not most, can afford no advance at all. Although this is a definite "con" for the freelance, there are "pros" to offset it. Chief among these are:

1. Advance aside, the author often gets a much better deal.
2. The author is assured of careful, concerned editing and helpful counsel.
3. The editor, who often doubles as publisher, puts heart, soul, and guts into the enterprise since both gratification and survival depend on the book's success.

A fast-moving book I once sold to a megapublisher was published exactly as I had submitted it. No contact at all with the editor, no suggestions for improvement. Okay, I'm a competent writer, but a book submitted with no ideas for improvement. I'm not that good. Obviously, the editor was too pressured and busy to spend time on my manuscript when he had more important matters to deal with. In dealing with the little guy, each and every contracted book is of the utmost importance.

This book you are now reading was submitted first by an agent to several megapublishers. It was held under consideration for four months by one of them before, after repeated committee meetings, being turned down. I finally submitted it on my own to Blue Heron where my proposal was accepted. I received caring personalized attention by the publisher who clearly has at much at stake in the book's success as I do. Offsetting the absence of an advance, I received a favorable contract with royalty and rights provisions better than most of the majors would have offered. I also received valuable insights and advice helpful in strengthening the book.

Labor of love

A recent article by Associated Press writer Dale Hopper is headed, *Small publishers do it for love, not money.* "Shoestring operations took off," writes Hopper, "when desktop publishing became profitable in the early '80s." Small publishers survive on smart salesmanship and promotion. They use direct marketing, trade shows, newsletters, and the Internet to sell books. They use distributors to access large booksellers who don't want to deal with thousands of publishers."

Can a book published by a small house pay off for the freelance seeking financial independence. Occasionally, in spades! Hopper cites on example: Connecticut columnist Sandi Kahn Shelton, whose book, *You Might As Well Laugh,* was published and marketed by Baltimore's Bancroft Press, and was a featured selection of the Literary Guild and Doubleday Book Club. That sounds very much like money in addition to love.

This book's publisher, Dennis Stovall, has his own success stories to tell: *Fight Club,* Chuck Palahniuk's novel has been picked up as a major feature film starring Brad Pitt. And Norton since purchased two more of his novels. Any wonder he quit his day job as a technical writer. *Nonfiction Book Proposals Anybody Can Write* racked up decent if not astronomical sales, was picked up by Writers Digest Book Club, and as a by-product plus yielded significant annual speaking fees. It is also worth noting that, on top of other benefits, a sale to the right independent can open the door to the majors.

Megapublishers buy—chiefly by committee consensus—books that fit well into preset computer-generated genre categories. Many genres, quirky, offbeat, too literary, whatever, simply don't qualify as mass audience potential. Yet they do have a market, in some cases perhaps thousands instead of millions of potential readers. But any books that should be published—meaningful contributions to knowledge, literature, art—are not published because they get turned down, not necessarily by editors, but by corporate financial and marketing types who influence buying decisions. I have no beef with the profit motive and dollar-centered decision making, but there should be alternatives as well for lesser mortals who are more art than genre focused.

I recall vividly a lunch meeting with William Morrow & Co. Senior Editor Howard Cady—the editor who boiled down Leon Uris's submission of about 3,000 pages, enough for three or four books, into bestselling *Exodus*. Howard, who became a good friend and helped me with the novel I am still trying to sell, mournfully lamented the literature-blasting effects of the Great Merger Movement. Another editor I know, her frustration level undisguised, confessed to me at an ASJA meeting, "I've become a veritable hack since committees took over my thinking for me."

Still, the old "silver linings" saw applies well here. The consolidation of scores of medium and large publishers into a relative handful of corporate giants served to spawn the growth of many countless small publishing enterprises headed by dedicated pioneers and risk takers like Blue Heron's Dennis Stovall, recent Baltimore start-up Bancroft's Bruce Bortz, and self-publisher Eric Hammel of Pacifica Press, who echo Howard Cady's lament.

Today there are 10,000 serious independent publishers, says Jan Nathan, executive director of Publishers Marketing Association. Associated Press writer Hopper quotes Nathan's philosophy: "I have yet to meet a person who says, 'I have come into this business to make a million dollars.' They have information, and they want to share it. That's what separates this industry (of independents) from all others, and makes it such a joy."

And don't forget the niche market. What's your specialization: Raising sunflowers? Antiquing? Breeding bees? Repairing clocks? Entering marathons? Antigun or antiabortion? Whatever. Markets for books on special interests may run into the thousands instead of the millions that whet mega appetites. The trick here is to search for and find the smaller publishing firm with less lofty bottom line goals, with interests compatible with your own, and which is sufficiently motivated to take you on as a freelance.

"A rose is a rose is a rose"—not necessarily

Caution is the eldest child of wisdom.

Victor Hugo

When a freelance replaces caution and wariness with gullibility and wishful thinking, experience with an independent can be painful and costly. Grifters and chiselers contaminate every field of endeavor. Publishing is no exception. Shoestring operation is one thing, unscrupulous quite another. A successful freelance I know had a book on an offbeat subject she desperately wanted to see published. Her agent submitted it widely, but the book was turned down by the majors because it was judged an off-genre submission. Having exhausted the majors, she combed the list of minors for possible takers, willing to forgo the advance as a sacrifice to her "labor of love."

Oh happy day! She received a congratulatory phone call from a Canadian publisher, followed by a glowing letter of acceptance. This was accompanied by slickly produced jacket covers and blurbs from books already published. Also included in the package was a rundown of the publisher's operating policy. Here, she was shocked to find a statement that read, "The Author agrees to pay the Publisher $3,850 to offset a portion of the publisher's cost." This requirement would be waived for established authors, the statement added. As an ASJA member, the author was more than qualified.

The publisher ignored this contention and assured her that her contribution would represent but a small portion of anticipated income for her highly marketable book. She was fortunately savvy and sophisticated enough to see through this scam. The publisher was, obviously, nothing more than a subsidy, or vanity, house. Had she shelled out the $3,850, she later would have been bombarded with additional subsidy charges to cover unanticipated production problems.

This outfit was subsequently criminally charged by the authorities. Vanity publishers, not all of them crooked, derive their income from the money they charge authors to have their books published. We have no beef with such enterprises, so long as they clearly state what they are. However, subsidy publishers who pretend to be otherwise, should be given a wide berth by freelances, however desperate they may be to see their name on a book.

Do you need an agent?

More to the point: Does an agent need you? Play your cards right and the answer may be yes, because without authors, agents are out of business. But as a freelance, selecting an agent—and as an agent, deciding to represent an author—is not unlike entering into a marriage contract. If not ideally matched, the arrangement will go bust. I agree with the oft repeated statement that it can be harder to find the right agent than it is to find the right publisher. I have worked with five different agents to date and still don't know if I ever found the right one. I've sold more books without an agent than with. My customer book—the most lucrative to date—I sold on my own.

How do you go about getting an agent? First and foremost, if you're not yet established with good credentials and an impressive track record, it may be tough if not impossible—except for agents who charge reading fees and get much if not most of their income from this source. Hook up with one of these guys and what you probably buy, and overpay for, is a short critique of your work.

Another way to attract a reputable agent is with exclusive subject matter so compelling, earth shattering, and unique it will be hard to resist. This must be real, not imagined. Unfortunately, if you are unknown, your own dramatic life or war experience will be of little interest to the reading public generally and to money-centered literary agents in particular. On the other hand, do you have new and exciting inside information about a celebrity? Can you link up with a doctor or scientist who has come up with a breakthrough cure for cancer, diabetes, or MS? Are you a former corporate, government, or HMO employee with information about shenanigans so shocking they would make Mike Wallace drool? Are you in a position to coauthor with, or ghost write a book for, a high profile celebrity? If so, an agent may welcome you warmly.

Literary agents are rarely interested in works shorter than books or films, so if you are thinking of an agent for articles, short stories, or poems, you are probably wasting your time. Even a hefty $3,000 article fee, for example, yields a commission too small for most agents to bother with, in addition to which their contacts are mainly book and not magazine publishers.

What can the right agent do for you?

A great deal, which is precisely what you should receive for parting with, typically, fifteen percent of the book income you earn. Here's a rundown of benefits you should expect from your agent:

- § PROFESSIONAL CRITICAL EVALUATION of your work. Many if not most agents are former editors, writers, or both. A good agent is chronically rushed, pressured, and behind schedule. The temptation is always present with a proposal that may not be earth shattering, but might result in a sale, to simply send it out as is to editors and hope for the best. For your 15 percent, you should get more than this.
- § GUIDANCE IN PREPARING AND REVISING not only the manuscript, but the book as well. From a marketing standpoint, in this day and age, the proposal is as important as the manuscript itself. Your book's fine writing and message may qualify it for awards, an appearance on the "Today" show or Oprah, and bestseller status. But if the proposal doesn't work, it won't sell.
- § REASONABLY FREQUENT COMMUNICATION. Sure, recognize and appreciate the agent's busy and pressured schedule. Also, that time spent communicating with authors is time away from communicating with editors. But a freelance should be kept informed about editorial response to work submitted, if not by the agent in person, by a secretary or aide.
- § A CARING, PERSONALIZED RELATIONSHIP. Agents should show more than routine, mechanical interest in their authors. One freelance told me, "If my agent hadn't held my hand over months of grueling experience with this book, I think I would have thrown in the sponge long ago."
- § MARKETING INFORMATION. Editors are well placed to know, from a subject point of view, what is in demand at a given time, what has been overexposed, and what up and coming trends might be pertinent.
- § REFERRALS. Editors in the market for particular books often confide their needs to agents they favor and rely upon. An agent with good contacts hears of book opportunities from

time to time, recommends authors who are hopefully qualified, and takes steps to get the two parties together. Two of my most successful books came into being this way.
- § EFFECTIVE NEGOTIATING. Competent as I believe myself to be as a writer, I also think I'm a lousy negotiator. When, hopefully, contract time rolls around, I feel my agent is much better placed, psychologically and otherwise, to negotiate the best possible deal. Agents understand better than most authors how the market stands at the moment and what the book in question is worth to the publisher, and what it will or won't go for.

So, assuming you are qualified and well established enough to interest a reputable agent in your work, is an agent for you? Maybe yes, maybe no. Run down the above list of potential benefits, and try to balance the scale. Are one or more or these services worth the fifteen percent of revenues dealing with an agent will buy?

The (nonfiction) book proposal

Every agent I ever met or heard speak agrees on the critical importance of a well structured proposal, preferably bound, that sells, not only the book, but its market potential, and the author as well. Here, in a nutshell, are the ingredients of a professional book proposal.

1. GOOD PROVOCATIVE TITLE. One that defines the book's content and makes the viewer want to see more.
2. PROFESSIONALLY DESIGNED COVER. Graphics and color usually help.
3. SYNOPSIS. This should briefly spell out the book's content, its main points and highlights and how readers can apply them to advantage. Notes New York agent Sheree Bykofsky "The single worst mistake writers make in book proposals is taking too long to get to the point. The book should be described concisely in the first or second paragraph."
4. THE PROPOSAL CONTENTS. With proposal page number for each feature identified.
5. THE BOOK. A somewhat longer rundown highlighting the book's uniqueness and pinpointing how it will help readers solve problems and fulfill their needs.

6. SPECIFICATIONS. Projected book length and delivery date. Proposed computer-related technology defining options for composing and submitting the book's chapters: Word processor, email, etc.
7. THE BOOK'S MARKET POTENTIAL. Projected readership and size, broken down by audience categories if applicable, and library purchase potential. Any special contacts or skills you may have to help market the book.
8. THE COMPETITION. A significant listing of books on the market, say ten or twelve, that will compete with your own book, with brief comments about each, and what makes your submission more beneficial and unique. Your main goal is to avoid comments like, "Oh no, not another book on the values of vitamins!"
9. AUTHOR PROFILE. Who you are, your credentials, and why you are uniquely qualified to write this book. Your education, background, and experience. This is no place to be shy. Include a rundown of published books, and articles, etc. on the specialization at hand and other subjects, along with favorable reviews and critical quotes. If you won awards, cite them. Include clips of articles and other work, and testimonials about how great you are. The more credentials that enhance your pro image, the better.
10. THE BOOK'S CONTENTS. Broken down chapter by chapter, with the highlights of what you plan to include. Well beyond a single page "Table of Contents."
11. CHAPTER SUMMARIES. A brief, easy-to-read synopsis of each chapter. Perhaps with an interesting anecdote or quote included to indicate how readers' problems will be solved and needs fulfilled.
12. A SAMPLE CHAPTER OR TWO. The strongest and most effective ones that best sell the book.

As you can see, a book proposal is not something you dash off. Roughly, in my experience, the time commitment for a professional proposal is about as much as it would be to research and write a couple of full length feature articles. But, apart from its function of actually selling the book, it is one of the most useful organizational tools I could name. Well structured chapter summaries, in particular, constitute a comprehensive outline so that, when the time comes, you can go about the business of writing the book in a well-organized, step-by-step way, with much of the grunt work already completed.

EIGHT

Love it, or leave it

Nine times out of ten if you don't like what you're doing, you should be doing something else.

Madeleine Payamps

No writer I know ever said writing was an easy way to earn a buck. As a freelance, no one has to tell you that the stress and strain of learning your trade alone can take hard and painful years. Even when established as a pro, challenges range from the mastery of salesmanship and meeting seemingly impossible deadlines, to dealing with a deadbeat editor or two along the way.

Why then do so many freelances persist in treading this pitted and rock-strewn road? Or, put another way:

What, more than anything, motivates you to stick to it?

Searching for answers to this question, I interviewed several writers and tried to probe my own depths as well.

Getting your message across

I suspect that many freelances, like myself, could cite more than one motivational trigger to explain why they persist as writers rather than choosing an easier way to make a living. Attempting to dredge up my own motives, the following drivers come to mind:

§ The money making potential I believe freelancing affords.
§ The diversity of interests freelance writers enjoy.
§ The chance to be my own boss and choose my own way of doing things.
§ Freedom from being chained to a desk. Interaction with other writers, editors, and research sources.

- Built-in flexibility. The option to set my own working hours and schedule.
- The satisfaction of, not always, but at least sometimes, achieving a goal of excellence in the work I turn out.
- Finally, and perhaps most important, getting across what I believe to be a meaningful and deeply felt message to my readers.

The message as motivator

As a management specialist, I have long crusaded for fair and equal treatment of employees regardless of race, religion, point of origin, age, gender, physical capability, or political persuasion. Having put in years on the corporate scene, and following that, on assignments for consultants, I encountered repeated examples of employee abuse and mistreatment. Years of experience and an abundance of evidence has long since convinced me that bigotry, intolerance, racism, hatred, and greed not only poison organizations but inhibit the spiritual and material growth of abusers as well.

That message, summed up in my William Morrow book, *Sure Fail—the Art of Mismanagement*, reads: "The organizational thrust these days is toward more productivity—more mileage per person, more return on the buck, increased output per dollar invested... An endless number of techniques and programs have been dreamed up with this objective in mind. But in my experience simply treating people like people will outperform every scheme ever devised for boosting output per person and will help avoid blunders that result in profit erosion."

This deeply felt conviction has been repeated often in one way or another in books, booklets, articles, and magazine columns I've written. I feel that if I can get across to readers that bigoted, hateful, and unfair treatment is not only mean-spirited and cruel, but hurts bigots as much as or more than their victims, I will have accomplished something worthwhile as a writer. I don't know how many people have been positively influenced by my message. But there's one thing I do know. If here and there it has helped to make a better person of someone, or improve the lot of some victim of prejudice, then I have chosen the right profession.

I know too that I'm not alone in this feeling. Writer-marketing executive Robert E. Levinson, who wrote four well received books and innumerable articles, has lived a richly rewarding and productive life. He told me recently, "I look upon writing as a moral obligation, a form of payback. I've developed ideas and concepts that helped enrich my life both spiritually and materially. I feel obligated to share them with others."

Bob, now in his 70's, has a longstanding aversion to retirement. He views it as a nasty word he would love to change to re-FIRE-ment. He is saddened by the millions of people who, after years of productive employment, "piss away" precious hours of life's balance killing time as couch or poolside potatoes, or engaging in other forms of boring inactivity. Directed mainly at a '50s and early '60s audience, the book Bob is currently writing is titled *Come Alive at Sixty-five*, with the message summed up its title. "For millions of healthy people," Bob says, "the years past so-called middle age should be the happiest and most productive of all. The more people I can persuade to 'come alive,' the more useful my payback will be."

ASJA member Morton Walker, a doctor of podiatric medicine, has recently had—hold on to your shoehorn—his 73rd book published. In addition to 2,250 articles (his count). "What impels me to keep writing," he says, "is an abiding interest in complementary medicine as the answer to humankind's ills." Ample payment, he feels, for all the research and hard work. That plus his love of good writing.

In chapter two I discussed ASJA member Richard M. Stapleton's unique specialization, lead poisoning. Dick, whose son is a himself a victim of this fearful hazard, urges readers: Stop poisoning your children. He spells out in detail to parents and website visitors how and what can be done to safeguard their children against this dread affliction. Feedback from his website and informative book, *Lead Is a Silent Hazard,* has helped to avert thousands of tragedies. Clearly, this gifted writer couldn't be more passionately dedicated to getting his message across. As one freelance put it to me, "What could make writing more worthwhile than helping thousands of people?"

When you care, you're ahead of the game

The freelance community's consensus is total: Your writing is best when it deals with what you care about most. This applies not only to writing but to any job you could name from accountant to zoo keeper. Nothing sparks performance more than deep concern about one's work.

"What more than anything motivates you to stick to this business?" When I asked Great Neck, New York freelance Murray Polner this question, he replied, "I write about issues and people that matter a great deal to me. I am deeply concerned with the Jewish experience in the U.S. and thus explored the life of rabbis in this country because there were so few books devoted to what they actually do."

Following through on the same specialization, he edited a volume of significant 20th Century Jewish personalities and institutions, and coedited a book on *The Challenge of Shalom: The Jewish Tradition of Peace and Justice*, and more.

No law says you must confine your caring to a single issue. Fascinated by baseball and the Brooklyn Dodgers, Polner says, he wrote a biography of Branch Rickey, the imaginative executive who brought Jackie Robinson and other African Americans into the previously all-white American pastime.

He also wrote and edited two books and coauthored a third book dealing with the Vietnam war in which he expressed his deep concern over what he perceived as "a whole generation badly used by their politicians." He concluded one book with these words: "Never before in American history have as many loyal and brave young men been as shabbily treated by the government that sent them to war; never before have so many of them questioned as much, as these veterans have, the essential rightness of what they were forced to do."

It is writing about issues that need to be written about, Polner believes, that makes freelancing, however difficult, worthwhile.

Thumbing through ASJA's membership directory that lists 1000+ writers, along with their specializations, profiles, and awards, it's no surprise to me that a fair number could be justifiably identified as "crusaders" covering one field or another. This listing represents many of the nation's most successful and prosperous authors, proof enough that when you care, you succeed.

Writers' motivators are as varied as the projects they tackle. From one interviewee comes this gloomy response. "For me, more than anything, writing is an escape—from family illness, marital hassles, problems with the kids, and this messed up world in general. Take away my word processor and I'd be climbing the walls."

Still another, now pushing eighty, told me, "Being downsized from a corporate writing job twenty years ago was the best thing that ever happened to me. I've been freelancing ever since and, almost from the outset, felt more psychologically and financially secure than I ever did chained to a desk. Today I put in about twenty hours a week and work at stuff I do best and enjoy most without having to drudge it out on repetitive boring assignments."

Don't settle for "competent"

If your ultimate goal is *Financial Independence as a Freelance*, I know of no more surefire strategy for success than becoming the best in your field, or as close to it as you possibly can. Not merely competent, but super-competent. Build a better microwave, tennis racquet, coffee maker, or pencil sharpener and the orders will keep pouring in. Write a better article, book, brochure, or executive speech and the same thing will occur.

The most successful writers I know are those who are least easily satisfied with the extent of their knowledge and the quality of their work. However good they may be, they constantly strive to do better. The rationale doesn't lend itself to dispute. Stand out from the crowd and you'll be noticed. This applies no less in writing than it does in politics, academics, or on the corporate scene.

If you're merely judged "competent" by editors you may get routine assignments. But if you rate "tops in your field," you'll get the juicy money-maker gigs the competition is clamoring for.

I know a freelance who serves as a stringer for PR firms, ad agencies, and corporate PR departments. A former ad agency staffer, he specializes in press releases and gets calls from sources when they're understaffed and backlogged with work. He's been doing this for years and barely manages to scrape by. He's regarded as "competent" to produce routine press releases, but not competent enough to be given more lucrative speech or article assignments. If he continues this way, he may continue to survive, but financial independence will never be within his grasp.

A top pro whose annual freelance income exceeds $200,000 told me recently, "Damn right I'm good! But I'm not good enough, and never will be, to satisfy myself. When I become complacent about the way I write, I'll probably start going downhill."

The trick, he said, is to improve and keep improving.

Improvement tip 1

My little brown loose leaf notebook has been near at hand for more years than I care to remember. It consists of two sections:

1. Words I run across in reading or listening that I should know the meaning of but don't. I look up the definitions and enter

them. Reviewing their meanings again and again helps to fix them in memory, making the words usable parts of my vocabulary.
2. Words and phrases that are particularly clever, apt, and out-of-the-ordinary ways of expressing thoughts and ideas. After repetitive review I claim these gems as my own. For example: Given the right situation, I might find it more effective to write, "He was totally flummoxed…" than "He was all mixed up." Or, "She hadn't a soupçon of evidence…" instead of, "She had no evidence…" Or, in place of "His reply made her think of something…" "His reply triggered a thought…" Get the idea? So why not start your own "little brown book" if you haven't done so already. Actually, green might serve just as well.

Improvement tip 2

Why do some writers win assignments from highly rated and top paying publications, or become nationally known columnists, while others must settle for lesser assignments? Study the prose of the super pros and find out. Pinpoint the stars you admire most, and analyze why you admire them. The harder you work at it, the more successful you will be. I have been emulating top earners—feature writers and columnists from *Newsweek* and *Time,* for example—since my early days as a freelance and I'm still doing it. My rationale: You are never so good that you can't get better.

Sure, subject matter is critical. The hotter the topic, the greater the demand. The more limited your audience, the less your chance to inhabit Bigbucksville. But equally important, apart from subject interest, is the quality of writing itself. The most outstanding characteristic of top paying prose is uniqueness. No question, it takes hard work, hard thought, and giving your imagination free rein to distinguish your prose from the ordinary and hammer across most provocatively what you are trying to say. Workhorses finish first. Benjamin Franklin agreed. "Work as if you were to live to be 100 years," he wrote. "Pray as if you were to die tomorrow." Work hard and your prayers may be answered.

QUESTION: Why do so many successful doctors and lawyers make it big as fiction and nonfiction writers?

My theory: One has to work one's butt off to be a successful lawyer or doctor. No less so to be a successful writer. Those guys have gotten into the habit. If you chose writing because you thought it would be easy, think again.

Experience the joy of writing

There is a happiness that comes from creative effort. The joy of dreaming, creating, building, whether in painting a picture, writing an epic, singing a song, composing a symphony...

Henry Miller

Okay, you may not get the same thrill and level of exultation from writing a top quality article or nonfiction book that masters like Tolstoy, Melville, and Hemingway must have derived from great works like *War and Peace*, *Moby Dick*, and *A Farewell To Arms*. Or that Gershwin got from "Porgy and Bess." Still, there's a payoff beyond cash for the years of tough knocks one endures to qualify as a pro. Don't sell the joys of excellent writing of any kind short. For one, there's the ego nourishment of knowing deep inside your gut that you're among the best in your field, whether it's a narrowly specialized genre like bird watching or aeronautical engineering, or a more general area like management or health. For another, there's the feeling you get when you're hard at it and the work is going really well. The prose gushes out in a kind of magical stream that flows on and on and enables you to turn out double or more of your normal output for minutes or hours on end. It may not happen often, but when it does I can tell you there is no feeling quite like it. It is suddenly worth all that butt-busting effort.

Find yourself a harsh critic

During much of my writing career I had the good fortune to work with, or for, people who were themselves top professionals. Burt Holtje, Rick Dunn, Wilbur Cross, Dick Conarroe, Howard Cady, Dennis Stovall, and others.

In the '50s and '60s I was part of a writers group that met weekly in Greenwich Village in a room at the back of a beauty parlor that we rented for a pittance. We took turns in reading each other's fiction and nonfiction masterpieces aloud and, in a no-feelings-spared spirit, had them mercilessly ripped apart by fellow critics. The advice wasn't always good or even justified, but that too was part of the learning experience—learning to skim the sesame seeds from the bagel. Mostly, those sessions didn't teach me how to write, they taught me how not to write, how to evaluate my work, how to pinpoint the mistakes I had made, and how to avoid repeating them.

I already mentioned one member of that group, a talented writer of fiction who went on to win numerous awards, write for top TV networks, and get nominated for an Emmy. Cal Clements, (now deceased) and I used to go for "coffee-and…" after group meetings to trade critiques of each other's work. Cal had a marvelously objective perspective. I got the best of the bargain by far. There's nothing like having your work pre-edited by a pro. Cal played the role of harsh editor and became one of the best friends I ever had. We often visited each other cross-country from California to Florida and could yak for hours on end. Oh my, those were the days!

It makes good morale and income boosting sense to find yourself a tough critic or two and enter into a mutual assistance pact with them. It could be freelance friends you already have, or writers you run into at a meeting of that writers' group you're going to join if you haven't done so as yet. Your shared goal is, as objectively as possible, to critique each other's work—as if you were the editor who must decide whether or not to buy the story, article, or book. What to do when flaws and flubs are uncovered? As Cal used to say, "You don't have to agree with me, but it should sure as hell give you something to think about."

Fall in Love With Your Work

The magic key to financial independence:

> The more you write, the better you get.
> The better you get, the more you enjoy what you do.
> The more you like what you do, the better you do it.
> The better you do it, the more you get paid.

My friend Jerry is a world class saxophone player. He makes a comfortable living blowing his horn and teaching kids how to play. He'd rather have a sax in his hands than a Rolls in his garage. Although financial independence is the last thing on his mind, Jerry's one of the happiest people I know. "I'm really blessed," he told me. "What could be better? Loving what you do, and getting paid to do it." Jerry loves playing so much, he does almost as many freebees as paid gigs.

Paul, a tennis pro I know, is a dyed in the wool aficionado. Same thing for my computer guru. Whatever your occupation—fixing clocks or freelance writing—loving what you do, and doing it over and over again, better and better each time, can't help but make you the best, and once you're the best you have it made.

Where do you come from?

As a freelance, are you cashing in on all you know and on all your experience?

If not, you may be missing out on specialization bonanzas that could put you decimal places ahead toward achieving your ultimate goal of financial independence.

Specializations develop, not only from work experience but from writing and research engagement as well. Do enough books on almost any given subject, and you'll automatically become a specialist. What follows is a brief rundown of some of my own specializations, how they came about, and how specialization pays off.

§ LABOR RELATIONS. My job experience, mainly as Systems Director for Fabergé Perfumes Inc. in New Jersey, often involved me in the resolution of employee problems, disagreements, and conflicts. As a manager I participated in arbitration sessions set up to settle grievances of one kind or another. One day I received a call from Dr. Lawrence Stessin, a management professor and publisher for whom I had done some work. He had been asked by *Plant Engineering* magazine if he might like to do a column on labor relations. Too busy at the time, he asked me if I would be interested. I most certainly was. This led to my column, "The Human Side of Engineering" which I have been writing for thirty years. It is one of my most enjoyable and financially lucrative assignments.

§ CUSTOMER SERVICE AND SALESMANSHIP. As a corporate middle manager I was strongly focused on customer satisfaction as a critical element of profitability. Dealing person-to-person with customers helped enhance my understanding of and sensitivity to customer needs. Early field experience selling leather goods, along with a brief retail sales stint, provided insights into how to sell effectively. This specialization led to bylined and ghosted assignments, a mail order bestseller on customer service, and innumerable articles and features on selling and customer service.

§ DATA PROCESSING. My Army experience supervising an electronic data processing installation proved invaluable in, first, landing me an EDP job after my discharge from the service. Then my combined experience from these jobs qualified me to produce several articles and a lucrative ghostwritten book on the subject.

§ PLANT AND OFFICE SECURITY. Early on in my writing career, I answered a *New York Times* help wanted ad for a writer and got the job. It was for a cheapo security firm that specialized in exploitation of its employees. After a six month stint I quit and have been a full-time freelance ever since. However, the experience gave me insights into the security business that provided material for several writing assignments on the subject for both magazines and competitive security firms.

A young man I know (I'll call him Bill) spent six years as production manager in a shoe manufacturing plant, having worked himself up from a routine line job. He confided in me that he hates his job "with a venom." He dislikes supervising subordinates, many of whom work harder avoiding work than they do on their jobs. He detests having to violate rules of decency he believes in for the sake of corporate profits. He rails against unreasonable pressures and the long hours the job demands. He regrets the time squeeze that prohibits him from involving himself with his two kids and watching them grow up.

His father-in-law, an executive in a publishing firm, sympathized with his plight. He asked, "Are you good at your job?"

"Sure. How do you think I got to make manager?"

"So tell me this: What would you most rather be doing?"

Bill's brow creased into a frown. "I always wanted to write. In fact, I once wrote a few short stories. Some of the response I got was encouraging. But no takers. I soon abandoned that dream."

The older man nodded thoughtfully. "Do you have any idea what the market is for short stories these days?"

Bill smiled sheepishly. "I guess I found out the hard way."

His father-in-law nodded. "Okay, you want to write? So write."

"About what?"

"About what you know. Management. Production. Manufacturing. Start with the trades; they're hungry for articles from knowledgeable people in the field. They don't pay much, but it's a way to break in, build a reputation, develop an image."

Bill didn't hide his skepticism. "How can I possibly support—"

"—You can't. I'm not suggesting you quit your job, at least not yet. But in time you may be able to."

Bill, now 32, is still employed as a production manager, and hates his job no less than ever. But a hard and dedicated worker, he already has had several articles published, recently signed a book contract, and has a second book proposal in the hands of a literary agent who is interested in his work. It would seem he's on his way.

Full-time or part-time?

Bill's story makes a critical point. No law says that as a freelance you can't be simultaneously employed on a job. That's the way I got started. It's the way thousands of freelances get started.

Running and marathon specialist Hal Higdon, whose freelance books and articles yield a respectable income, doubles as a senior writer for *Runner's World*. A marathoner himself, he also serves as a training consultant for the LaSalle Bank's Chicago Marathon.

Scores of doctors and lawyers, on and off the bestseller lists, haven't stopped doctoring and lawyering. But for whatever reasons of their own— ego nourishment, release from the stress and strain, relaxation and fun—they freelance part-time.

Part-time employment can be a virtual necessity early on in one's freelance career, especially when family responsibilities intrude. In my own case, I made the transition by obtaining a part-time writing job for a small PR firm three days a week before quitting my full-time job as a data processing manager. I gradually whittled this down to two days a week. Finally, having acquired a couple of PR accounts of my own, I decided to hit the freelance road full-time. I left the PR firm and continued to serve it as account executive on an ad hoc basis. As in many enterprises, step-at-a-time is the key.

Point two, courtesy of our friend Bill, is equally potent: It's the not uncommon realization that the job you hate, when viewed from a writer's objective, often takes on a whole different perspective. Bill, who still dislikes the pressures and grind of supervising people, confessed to me that although he dislikes the business, he enjoys writing about it.

"For one thing," he says, "while my ideas for improving the workplace and worker morale are largely ignored by upper management, my editors love them. In writing, the only constraints I face are the reader-related ones of the publication for which I'm working. Smart editors know that the more leeway they give writers to express themselves freely, the better and more useful the product will be."

Tapering down

Whatever your present age, if there is any time when you will most appreciate being a writer, it is when you reach 60 plus. I speak from experience. Let's, assume, you're not ready yet to throw in the career sponge. Assume too that, like millions of people at this point in their lives, on the one hand, you don't want to retire (hated word); but on the other, you wouldn't mind tapering down. Employed at a job, this may not be so easy. On top of which, there's always the specter of being downsized to worry about. Not so if you're a freelance.

I couldn't begin to estimate how many people have told me how lucky I am. "You can work whenever you want, as much as you want, and on whatever you want."

Right on! When I count my blessings, this one is way up near the top of my list.

The bonanza advantage

While counting blessings, I don't want to overlook the Bonanza Advantage. For one thing, it makes life more exciting; for another, it makes freelancing more profitable.

Norman Mailer was right on target when he wrote, "Boredom slays more of existence than war." How many people find their jobs boring? Millions? Or is this an understatement? Routine jobs, even so-called higher level jobs, necessarily involve day-to-day, week-to-week, month-to-month repetition and sameness. Much less so for the freelance. Few workers are more blessed by diversity, which no one has to tell you, is the best prescription for overcoming boredom.

The Bonanza Advantage refers to a windfall that can be as unexpected as a Florida snowstorm in July. The corporate counterpart might be an unanticipated bonus for a manager or technologist. It happens rarely if ever in business; not often, but at least occasionally, in freelancing. When a bonanza strikes, in my experience, it can keep your morale up for weeks. Here's a sampling of what I'm talking about.

SPEAKING ENGAGEMENT—Many writers get multiple mileage from their work by taking advantage of lecture opportunities. More comfortable at the word processor, I never pursued this form of supplementary income. Then one day, out of the blue as they say, I got a call from a former editor, Howard Cady at William Morrow. "Ray, how would you like to talk before the New York State Realtors Association at the Concord Hotel. Pick any one of your books that you wish. You get a freebee weekend for you and your wife, and there's a modest stipend involved." The Concord was at the time a pricey resort in the Catskills. My wife and I were thrilled at the offer. I selected walking as the subject of my talk. We were treated graciously by the Realtors, who purchased several of my books (*The Complete Book of Walking*) at the end of my spiel. It was a fun experience, good training for subsequent TV promotional appearances, and I got paid in the bargain.

BESTSELLER—As any editor could confirm, book publishing is often a hit-or-miss venture at best. Of my twenty-seven published books, a few did fairly well, others bombed, two did quite well, and one...! Well, when I learned from Dartnell, that my book on customer service had turned into a direct mail bestseller, it substantially boosted my income for years, and heightened my appreciation of the Bonanza Advantage.

"SLOW POISON"—Several years ago I was a regular contributor to publishers that produced "rack booklets" sold to corporations which placed them on racks in the cafeteria or lobby for distribution to employees. These normally yielded an income of $200 to $400 each in either flat fee or royalty. Uninspiring, but it was steady work. The Bonanza Advantage occurred when

I was notified by publisher John Beckley of Economics Press that my booklet, "Slow Poison," on the devastation of, and cure for, anger, had been picked up by General Motors with its million or so employees. Totally unexpected, royalties exceeded $1,500, respectable money in those days.

ONE PHONE CALL—This dates back thirty years or so. I received the phone call from Professor Lawrence Stessin, previously referred to, that led to the acceptance of my proposed column, "The Human Side of Engineering," by *Plant Engineering* magazine that so greatly enhanced the enjoyment of my work and my earnings over the years. The Bonanza Advantage! Sometimes all it takes is one phone call.

ONE MESSAGE—Sometimes all it takes is one message—one email message. Again—"out of the blue'—the editor/publisher of a leading marketing and sales magazine, recently emailed me an invitation to write for her. I had no idea where she got my name. I still don't know. But the communication and subsequent assignments—exclusively by email—were rewarding, enjoyable, and right down my proverbial alley.

DOUBLE PAY—As an employee, how often do you receive duplicate paychecks?

The typical reply would be never. As a freelance I received duplicate payments on three separate occasions. Once for $1,800, once for $2,500, once for $1,200. Each time I promptly returned the extra check. One client called to thank me profusely. The other two clients—I could hardly believe it!—sent back the duplicate checks. One called to say it would be made it up with another assignment, then decided instead to "write it off" as a kind of bonus. The third client told me "to forget about it." He apparently preferred absorbing the extra cost to having his mistake called to light. I was uncomfortable with the decision, but learned long ago not to argue with a customer.

OFFBEAT DEALS—On the corporate scene you're boxed in by a rash of rules and protocols. Not so as a freelance. When my son, Ken, who lives and works in France, decided to visit with his wife and three kids, the problem was, Where would he stay? Our two bedroom Florida apartment was too small to put them up comfortably. Money was tight in those days. At the time, I was working on book number two for my favorite client, Bob Levinson, who owned three hotels in the area—two Holiday Inns and a Sheraton. I called Bob and proposed a barter deal: Put up my son and his family at your Fort Lauderdale Holiday Inn on the beach, and I'll make it up with equivalent writing service as compensation. Bob's reply was immediate. "Tell them to come on down." They had a great vacation, saved more than $2,000, and everybody was happy.

The Bonanza Advantage. Simply another diversity plus inherent to freelance enterprise. Boredomitis interruptus.

My son, the entrepreneur

I've held several jobs in my lifetime, from boring to relatively interesting. I've worked for good and bad bosses. One reason, probably the main reason, I don't feel any job I ever had holds a candle to freelancing is that as a freelance I'm in business for myself, an entrepreneur. On your own, you make the crucial decisions that affect you; you arrange your work schedule; you succeed or fail based on your own performance, not someone else's; you are beholden to no one but yourself.

As often happens with father and son, Ken's experience parallels my own. My restless son, who now lives in France, held writing and editorial jobs for the Associated Press, Radio Station WINS, *Business Week*, and others. After several months he reached this simple conclusion: What I'm doing for others I can do for myself. Put another way: Why share the rewards from your talent and productivity with an employer when you can have it all to yourself. Today, Ken runs a his own communications consulting firm (InterAngle) headquartered in Paris and, with top-rated clients, is doing quite well.

The decision takes guts. It's not easy to give up the security of a regular paycheck—sometimes the false security—to venture out on your own. But if, for one reason or another, you're unhappy working for someone else, the rationale may make sense.

It made sense to me decades ago when I quit a well paying job to freelance full-time. Win or lose, I reasoned, whatever my talent and productivity are worth, I don't need an employer skimming hard earned shekels off the top. Today, thousands of writers function as employees when they might be earning more and enjoying a lifestyle more to their liking self-employed. Are you one of them?

NINE

To market, to market

The key to success is not selling things, but selling yourself.

Dr. Albert Weggam

Wow, what a great idea! You're an antigun activist who enjoys big game hunting. So you've come up with this brainstorm for a book: *How to Hunt big Game With a Bow and Arrow!* Unique. Original. From a marketing standpoint, little if any competition. There's only one thing wrong: The potential market is meager or less.

Is this a nutcake idea or not? Sure is. But you'd be surprised at how many totally off-market queries and proposals publishers large and small receive every day. Their bulk could probably fill the Grand Canyon.

For freelances on a quest for financial independence, the following two words should be etched into their consciousness:

GET REAL!

The essential first step in selling a book, article, film—or any commercial product you could name—is to make sure it has a market large enough to more than cover the cost of creating, producing, packaging, merchandising, and promoting it. Step two, no less important, is to tailor your product to the specific need of the "customer" you hope to persuade that your product will fill that need better—more profitably and cost-effectively—than the hundreds of others competing for attention. Or, put another way: Know your market.

Know your market

I'll never forget the comment I received years ago from Lydia Strong when she was editor of *Management Review*, published by The American Management Association: "In my experience," she said, "the quickest turnoff—and it recurs repeatedly—is the query or proposal from writers who haven't done their homework. It's like the salesperson who calls on the glassware buyer with a line of aluminum pots." She added, "You wouldn't believe the mountain of stuff I get that isn't remotely appropriate to my purpose. I received a query just this morning that would have been more suitable for *Boy's Life* than *Management Review*."

Too many writers get a bright idea for a story, research the material, complete the manuscript and then search for an appropriate publisher. This may work for fiction but not nonfiction. The smart and more practical approach is to first investigate the market so that you will be in a position to tailor your material to the very special needs of the editor of your choice.

Editors of major publications receive mountains of email messages, letters, phone calls, and faxes each week. All wearily echo the same lament. "The most successful writers I know," editor after editor has told me, "are the ones who understand the markets they write for and know how to think like an editor."

How do good editors think? First and foremost, they get into the minds of their readers. With the help of polls and surveys, reader response, ongoing market analysis, and practiced savvy, they home in on readers' needs, desires, and interests. Their aim is to pinpoint the way their readers think and feel about what interests them most.

Richard R. Conarroe, a communications specialist whose multifaceted career has taken him to almost every journalistic niche you could think of from editor and publisher to producer and publicist, told me recently, "Editors are the busiest people I know. If you want them to love you, you have to make their lives easier. The best way to do this is by giving them exactly what they need when they need it."

Shots in the dark rarely hit

It makes no sense. A writer gets an idea for an article, spends days or weeks sweating over the manuscript, then sends it to an editor without first making the effort to define the publication's special needs. The shot-in-the-dark freelance reasons, for example, that the article idea is of interest to women, so out goes a query to a woman's magazine—or worse, the completed article—without consideration that every woman's magazine is in some way or other uniquely different from its competitors. The piece bounces back with a form rejection slip and gets mailed to the next woman's magazine listed in *Writer's Market* and so on down the line. Same procedure applies to virtually all publications whatever the genre. In freelancing, thinking generically rarely pays off; the operational mindset is specific.

Despite the self-defeating consequence of blind shooting, the tonnage of hit-or-miss manuscripts that load down mail delivery trucks daily could sink an ocean going vessel. It's all such a waste of time, money and effort, and all so unnecessary. Trust me. I learned this the hard way. In my early days the number of rejection slips I accumulated as feedback from hit-or-miss submissions could have wallpapered a good sized living room. The obvious conclusion: Why guess at a publication's unique subject and style requirements when, with so little effort you can pinpoint what is specifically needed?

Remember, it is to the editor's as well as your advantage to educate you regarding what is most salable. *New Choices* editor-in-chief Greg Daugherty, for example, guest-speaks periodically before writers groups in an effort to familiarize members with the magazine's readership and what he is most interested in. Chief coverage areas, he makes clear, are health, personal finance, and travel, and he makes clear that would-be contributors must have expertise on these subjects. He spells out in detail exactly what writers should shoot for and what they should avoid. Be upbeat, he advises, but not corny. Don't condescend to readers, and don't refer to them as "aging Baby Boomers," "mature," or "seniors." Shoot for information that will yield immediate reader benefit. Use real-life anecdotes and quote authoritative experts—but don't seek out celebrities. Strive for clarity, logical structure, and inspiration. Above all, study the magazine, and try to understand and reflect its tone.

How much more specific could you get? And think how much easier it is to adhere to this kind of guidance when it is right there in front of you.

WRITER'S GUIDELINES—One of most obvious ways to get the information you need to tailor your manuscript to the editor's needs is to simply request a set of publishing guidelines, enclosing a stamped self-addressed envelope (SASE) for response. Preparing a manuscript without guidelines is like rowing a boat without oars. In addition to subject, style, tone, length and other tips, guidelines usually clue in writers about which subject areas are open to freelances, which are not covered at all, and which are staff written.

Even easier than sending for guidelines via email or snail mail, if you own a computer, is to access the targeted publisher or publication on the Internet. Simply conduct your search by entering the web address. As an example, doing this chapter I keyed in *www.motherjones.com* and up popped the magazine's home page which informed me *Mother Jones* is a publication that features "social and political commentary from a left-of-center perspective." I was also able to review a list of published stories from current and back issues along with clues as to what's hot at the moment. As a freelance I was encouraged to email queries to: *query@motherjones.com*, but urged—What else?—"to first look at our writer's guidelines."

Assuming that I as a freelance wanted to contribute to *Mother Jones*, what else would I want to know? With precisely this question in mind, a section on the magazine's web site headed What We're Looking For included the following items:

§ Hard-hitting, investigative reports exposing government cover-ups, corporate malfeasance, scientific myopia, institutional fraud or hypocrisy, etc.
§ Thoughtful, provocative articles which challenge the conventional wisdom (on the right or the left) concerning issues of national importance.
§ Timely, people-oriented stories on issues such as the environment, labor, the media, health care, consumer protection and cultural trends.

So would it be worth a writer's time to send *Mother Jones* a query about an article on better parenting? No way!

A section headed "How to Query Us" states that telephone or faxed inquiries as well as unsolicited manuscripts or fiction are unacceptable. Freelances, are further instructed to explain in their queries what they expect to cover and the approach, tone, and style they plan to use. They are also informed that the editor would like to know their specific qualifications to write on the topic and what "ins" they might have with reliable sources. Wannabe contributors are asked, too, to provide full documentation so that their story can be fact-checked. And they are cautioned to keep the magazine's three-month lead time in mind, and spell out how their story will be different from others on the same topic. Finally, along with a self-addressed stamped envelope (SASE), the first-time contributor is asked to include two or three copies of previously published articles.

Clearly, the above information, thoughtfully considered, would frighten off many if not most would-be contributors. Clearly, too, those not frightened off would be the writers best qualified and most likely to succeed in establishing a working relationship with the editor. The choice is yours. What's preferable: To send a query or manuscript in the dark, violating one or more of the stated requirements and receiving a form rejection slip for your trouble? Or adhering to editorial needs as closely to the letter as possible, and standing a good chance at acceptance?

What, specifically, do editors look for in author queries? The following rundown of editorial comments on the subject will provide a few insights:

- § "Tell what the story is about in a straightforward way. Don't be your own publicist."
- § "Include a provocative lead that will grab my attention."
- § "Make it short and sweet; keep in mind that time is of the essence."
- § "Make me realize from your query that you devoted time and effort toward getting to know the magazine and its needs."
- § "Sell me on the uniqueness of your subject, treatment, or approach."
- § "Convince me you are qualified to write authoritatively on the subject."

Finally—one more time—if you are doing a book and want to narrow your chances from one in thousands to one in hundreds or less, consider submitting to small publishers instead of the majors. Once you're well established, you can shoot for the top. If you are planning a book, access the Publishers Marketing Association or AcqWeb on the web. (See Chapter 7) Scrolling down subject category listings—health, parenting, ecology, careers, etc.—you will quickly and easily zero in on publishers whose needs are most closely compatible with the particular subject you have in mind. With this information you will be in a position to tailor your query and proposal to the specific market in question. *Specific!* Burn that word into your consciousness.

Get to know the editor personally

In business as in life, the value of personal relationships could not be overstated.

The harder you work to understand the special needs, tone, and style of the publication you are targeting—and the more able you are to convince the editor of your professionalism—the more cooperative the editor will be in cooperating with you in your goal to become a contributor. Tough as it may be in some cases to bridge the gap between the form rejection slip and the explanatory editorial response, it's important to keep in mind that a magazine's (or publisher's) team of contributors constitutes the editor's main stock in trade. As a member of that team, you are just as important to the buyer as the buyer is to you.

How does one develop a personal relationship with an editor? By keeping in mind that with the possible exception of traders on the Exchange, editors are the busiest people alive, and by dreaming up ways to make the editorial job easier. Once you establish a relationship, if for some reason you can't accept an assignment, recommend a qualified writer who can if you know one. This favor will bounce back from two directions, and the more time you save for your editor, the more Brownie points you chalk up for yourself. What's in it for you? Recalling my own experience, more than once in a conversation with an editor, I was tipped off as to what was hot at the time. More than once, when an article that was rejected, a call to the editor spelled out precisely why it was rejected—wrong approach, timing not right, similar to another article on tap, etc.—so that I was able to fix it and sell the piece to someone else. And more than once, convert it with a rewrite into acceptance.

Pretend your name is on the masthead

Guidelines are invaluable, but guidelines alone aren't enough. When it comes to articles or magazine features the success key in working with editors is to project yourself mentally into staff membership. As a customer/selling specialist, I recently decided to take a crack at writing for a fine information-packed magazine called *Selling Power* with its impressive readership of salespeople and marketing executives. After studying the publication's guidelines, I obtained three copies of the magazine and read and reread the articles and features that particularly interested me. I studied the language, tone, style and approach. I concentrated hard to put myself in the minds of both subscriber and editor. I then made my pitch, emulating as closely as possible the content and format displayed in the book. It worked. I got the assignment and soon after my name appeared on the magazine's masthead. The key operational words? Concentration, and hard.

Working with agents—pros and cons

Some writers swear by literary agents; others swear at them. From the con side, deliberating whether or not an agent will benefit your career as a freelance, one thought to keep in mind is that, from the agent's perspective, an agent's loyalty is more likely to go to the editor than the writer. This common sense conclusion is supported by long years of experience. Editor contacts are bread and butter for agents. With one obvious exception: The bestselling author represents not only the bread and butter but the gravy as well. I have known agents who would sell Mom or Dad down the river to keep writers in their stable who repeatedly make the bestseller list.

Still in "con" territory, it has also been my experience that literary agents who charge reading fees are most commonly in the reading fee, as opposed to the agenting, business. They sell advice you can get from a good book on writing at a price that's substantially higher. Typically, too, the counsel is dispersed by college students or recent grads with no more field experience than the client. Over the years, I have been exposed to more than one wannabe freelance who would have been best advised not to quit their day job, or to choose another line of work. Typically, the aspiring freelance who deals with a reading-fee agent receives not only a manuscript critique—sometimes of questionable value—but hope-building encouragement as well. The "your work shows promise" message in a nutshell is, "Keep 'em coming" which, of course means keep the reading fees coming, tool.

One final "con" comment, then on to the good guys. Although I have in my career achieved financial independence as a freelance decades ago, I never enjoyed the good fortune to rank as the kind of star an agent would kill for. On the one hand, I had no trouble getting agents interested; on the other hand, the handful of agents I worked with over the years never regarded my association as an indispensable asset. The typical rationale regarding a manuscript: Looks like a possible; I'll take a shot at it. Thus, since good literary agents are about as time-pressured as editors, in at least two notable cases I found communicating with my agent of the moment regarding books of mine sent out to market a frustrating experience. Some agents do report on submissions fairly regularly if only by postcard. Others respond rarely if at all. More than once, it took two or three long distance calls on my part to elicit a response. In one memorable case in which I had submitted, at the agent's request, seven copies of the book proposal with virtually no feedback, I decided after a year or so to withdraw the manuscript and asked for the return of my proposals. The response was that they couldn't be found.

How often is too often to contact your agent regarding the status of your manuscript. "Too often," says Tom Fensch of the New Century agency, "is more than once every two-and-a-half weeks or so." One agent accommodatingly sent me a copy of every response she received from an editor. Increasingly these days agents prefer email correspondence to phone calls and faxes. If the office is efficiently run, a quick check of the computer data base makes response easy, painless, and inexpensive.

The good guys

Good agents can be worth their weight in royalty checks if hooked up with the right writer. Ideally, the agent you deal with as a freelance should be strong in the genre of your choice—strong meaning good editorial contacts in your field of specialization, editors who depend on him and rely on his judgment to fulfill their unique editorial requirements. As a freelance seeking representation, does it pay to hold out until you find an agent with contacts in your genre? Nancy Love who runs the agency bearing her name calls the question a no-brainer. She asks, "Would you go to an obstetrician if you were having trouble with your eyes?" The agent with a track record in your genre can cash in on that experience and connections to market your book most effectively.

In my experience good agents earn their commission—most commonly 15% of royalties and advance—in three highly significant ways:

1. GUIDANCE. I am currently agentless, but one agent I used had me revise my book proposal three times. His suggestions paid off in an eventual sale. Some of the best agents I know are former editors; a handful are competent writers. Most have been through the mill and back. The best of the lot—as opposed to their counterparts who do little more than send out

manuscripts as is—are able to evaluate writers work through the eyes of the editor most likely to buy it, and get you back on track if they stray.
2. NEGOTIATIONS. In many if not most cases an experienced agent will have a better feel than the writer for how much an editor is willing—and authorized—to spring for an advance on a book, and can negotiate a better deal on royalties, rights, and other contract clauses as well. This can, and often does, more than compensate for the hefty 15% commission usually charged.
3. HAND-HOLDING. The best agent-author relationships are those where the agent acts as a built-in comfort station for the freelance—lending encouragement in tough periods, providing a receptive ear when needed, applying strategies and techniques to break writers block if it becomes problematical. In more than one case I know, freelances rank agents among their very best friends.

Oft told tale

This horror story has been repeated so often it has become a cliché. You go through the torment and agitation of turning out and finally selling a book. You're dispatched on a promotional tour to several cities by your publisher. You do a score or more radio interviews. You appear as a guest on TV shows to enthusiastic audience response. Then finally—my God, finally!—pub date arrives. You race to the nearest Walden or Barnes & Noble bookstore to see how your book is doing and—you guessed it—your book it is not in the store. No sign of it. If you're lucky you may induce a clerk to check the storage room and find that the carton containing your brainchildren has not been unpacked. But more likely, it simply hasn't arrived for reasons unknown. "We've found that the bookstore always blames the publisher," Dennis Stovall says, "though we do all we can to remind them to order with time to spare."

Tearing out your hair won't help and will only damage your scalp. So what to do? Is it your agent's responsibility to make sure the books will be in the stores—especially following your TV appearance and the buy impulses it hopefully inspired. Unfortunately not. Notify your agent, of course, and the sooner the better, and get him to raise hell with the publisher. But most important, raise hell yourself, and keep raising hell until action is taken. Also, get the bookstore in on the act if you can. No one knows better than the manager that if the books aren't there he won't sell them. From Stovall, a final word of advice: "Authors should always carry a carton of books, just in case."

Publicizing your book

As a freelance what should your role be in publicizing your book? This is a tough question to answer. In a nutshell, it depends on your realistic expectations.

Do you really and truly believe that your brainchild has the potential to become a bestseller? Is your faith in its value, and your enthusiasm, so strong that you are willing to make a significant investment in time and money to promote it? Money? Darned right, money. Cash outlay aside—we'll get to that in a minute—for the freelance, time is money. When you're out promoting, you're not writing. The bottom line is: Is it realistic to expect that the number of books sold as a result of your promotional efforts, independent of the publisher's, will more than pay off your investment? If so, go for it, but keep the realities in mind.

My William Morrow book, *Sure Fail, the Art of Mismanagement*, was published some years ago to excellent reviews. It was cover-blurbed by Laurence Peter (*Peter Principle*) and other impressive names. The book barely broke even and drew an apology from my editor. "It should have been a bestseller," he said. "We let you down."

Or did I let myself down? I contacted a bunch of media people and initiated a number of TV appearances and radio interviews. But I didn't go "all out;" I didn't want to take the time away from my writing. Should I have? I don't know the answer.

What would have going "all out" entailed? Book signings all over the place; a national tour more extensive that what the publisher was willing to spring for; weeks devoted to little if anything else other than the book's promotion. Should I have hired my own publicist? Well reputed Barbara Monteiro, who runs a public relations firm in Manhattan, charges $5,000 a month for publicist services. In my book, that's steep. Financial independence is one thing, crap shooting another.

What can you expect from the publisher in the way of publicity? In my case, it wasn't much. For one thing, publication of *Sure Fail* coincided with the release of five or six books by celebrities. Dreyfack, not being a household name, occupied a back burner. I did make a few boy scout tries to contact

Morrow's publicist with suggestions and assurance of cooperation, but was unable to reach her. I later learned that two or three weeks after the book's release she either quit or was fired. Promotion during this critical period was nil. As a result, Dreyfack is still not a household name.

Author crusades

Stories are legend about writers, so inspired by and enamored of their brainchildren, and so sold on their book's potential, that—despite meager promotional outlay by the publisher—they embarked on one-man crusades to alert the world to its value. I think it was Wayne Dyer, if I recall correctly, who packed the back of his car with copies of *Your Erogenous Zones* and visited hundreds of bookstores nationwide to pitch the book. Entirely on his own, he promoted Zones into an unprecedented bestseller and multiplied his small advance into an astronomical figure and a green light for subsequent bestsellers.

Will it pay off for you to emulate Dyer. Sure! If… In fact, two "ifs." If your book's theme and message constitute a soul-inspired driving force in your life of such overriding importance that you are willing to invest weeks and months of your time, not to mention dollars, to promote it. As was the case for Dyer. And, no less important: If you are a dynamic super-salesperson, as talented and self-confident a pitchman as you are an author. I've seen and heard Wayne Dyer on television and elsewhere. Not that his book wasn't a great and inspiring read; it was. But this guy could sell beach umbrellas to Eskimos. Listening to his pitch, I couldn't wait to get my hands on the book. If these two "ifs" jell in your mind and your heart, by all means, go for it.

What about book signings at stores? It's a controversial subject. Some writers I've interviewed see them as a waste of time. Others are gung ho in favor. Opponents view the number of books sold at a signing as a grain of sand in a sandstorm. Advocates make the point that enough signings add up and take hold from a word-of-mouth standpoint. Major chains like Walden or Borders like authors to be available to give mini-lectures; work with them and they'll work with you. One freelance told me that "on more than one occasion" a book signing triggered spinoff media coverage and, in one case, a lucrative ghostwriting assignment.

On a cost-benefit basis, how does one measure values derived from a signing against the time and dollar investment? My calculator can't handle a question that complex.

The credibility roadblock

Nothing will trigger a form rejection slip faster than an editor's conclusion that the author lacks credibility. Your name is Jane F. Lance. You have a great idea for a book that gives parents valuable insights into dealing with teen age rebellion. You checked the bookshelves and decide your revelations are unique. An important plus. You're a darned good writer and you know it; published clips included with your proposal confirm it. Another important plus. You reviewed your material again and again and made certain you have enough for a book as opposed to a magazine article. You're still ahead. You got the word from people in the know that the subject is timely and leads rather than trails a trend, not one that would inspire an editor to conclude, "Oh no! Not another book on teen age rebellion." So far you're batting 1,000. You dreamed up a catchy and provocative title. You conclude you can't miss.

So what's the problem? The problem is credibility—the editor's voiced or unspoken conclusion: "Who the hell is Jane Lance? What qualifies her to write an authoritative book on parenting in general and teenage rebellion in particular? Your indignant response: "I'm a mom with two teen age kids!" Sorry, Jane. It ain't enough. What's your professional background? Are you a psychologist or shrink, or at the very least a professor or teacher? What other stuff have you done on the subject: books, articles, instruction manuals?

Editors receive untold numbers of manuscripts on any subject you could name from professionals in their specialized areas of expertise. The author who fails to qualify as a recognized expert on the subject in question doesn't stand a chance against the established professional. The conclusion is simple: You have this great idea for a book on how to deal with teenage rebellion. If you don't have the professional credits needed to impress an editor, either forget about the book or find a qualified expert to collaborate with you.

What about the web?

Is writing for the Internet an opportunity or crapshoot for the freelance? It depends. The first thing to keep in mind is that when you do business on the Internet you play in a different ballpark from any you have pitched balls in before. On the one hand, opportunities abound; on the other, writing for the Web can be risky.

On the opportunity side, there's an ever-growing demand for Web content. From the standpoint of risk, possible as it sometimes may be to be ripped off by a print publisher, it can be more so when the paymaster is the Internet. Dealing with print media, gauging the publication's size, longevity, corporate parent, and advertising, the freelance can get a relatively good reading on its financial credibility. Not necessarily so with Web sites on the Internet. While it can be assumed that the best known sites—Amazon, AOL, Apple, Corel, MSNBC, *NY Times,* etc., as well as major magazine and TV sites—are stable, hundreds of others are shaky at best. Web horror stories are at least as plentiful as those that are print-based.

How can you tell?

Most Web sites have an About Us button to click on. This often leads to a press release that describes funding, backing, and ownership. Also, a look at the site's content and credits will cite the names of contributors; the presence of known authors is one indication of financial credibility. Lacking the inclusion of a stable support group or proof of funding, writing for the Internet could be no more than a crapshoot.

Thousands of people these days, many of them wet-behind-the-ears kids, are planning to initiate Web sites and get rich in the process. Many are either underfunded or not funded at all. I personally can call to mind two sites run by experienced entrepreneurs, but backed by little more than self-confidence and their own limited resources, where freelance contributions are encouraged. I wouldn't touch either one of them with a 90-word-a-minute word processor.

What's the best way to break in?

Okay, you are relatively convinced that Iwantyourstuff.com is financially sound and you want to take a crack at its Web site. What now? Here's a brief rundown of questions to ponder:

- § Have you thoroughly researched and investigated the site?
- § Do you know others who contribute to it?
- § Are you impressed by the site's content? Does it relate to one or more of your writing specializations?

§ Are you clearly—professionally—qualified to contribute?
§ Does the site contain a substantial number of articles? If so, you can probably assume it uses freelance material.
§ Did you check out Tedesco's Guide to On-line Markets?
§ Will your contribution be a one-shotter? You're better off shooting for repeats that tie in with your specialization.
§ Finally, should you consider putting your book on someone's Web site? Think twice, then once again.

TEN

Step-by-step from the ground up

You can't do today's job with yesterday's methods and be in business tomorrow.

Nelson Jackson

NOTE: We learn from each other. A primary purpose of this chapter is to uncover bell ringers—match points between your background and experience and my own—and from the comparisons, to help you draw whatever activating conclusions you can. What follows is in a sense an Anatomy of a Writer for what you can glean out of it.

First, let's see if you have what it takes to achieve financial independence as a freelance writer? Hopefully, the following checklist will provide some insights. Most successful writers I know have certain characteristics in common. On a piece of scrap paper, place a checkmark for each of the traits that apply to you.

1. Writers hate the word "ordinary"; they are proud of being different.
2. Writers are free spirits, do not like being supervised and controlled.
3. They are imaginative and creative.
4. They are fiercely protective of their independence.
5. They are analytical, want to get at the underlying reasons.
7. They like to be up and around, not chained to a 9 to 5 desk.
8. They enjoy interacting with people.
9. They are proud of their profession and in need of recognition.
10. They are for the most part honest and ethical.

Total your checkmarks. If you checked eight or more of the above characteristics, you are to be either congratulated or sympathized with. You're a freelance writer at heart.

From novice to professional

My urge to write dates back as far as I can remember. In seventh grade I wrote a horror story that would have done Stephen King proud. My shortsighted English teacher scolded me for it. I was stunned but not thwarted.

Times were tough when I was a kid. After graduating high school I scoured *The New York Times* want ads and found ten times more ads for accountants than anything else. I got a job delivering textiles in New York's garment center and attended City College evenings where I majored in accounting. It took me four years to realize how much I hated accounting.

I switched my major to advertising and suffered a succession of deadly jobs—stockman, warehouseman, utility man, packer, machine operator in a defense plant. In my spare time I wrote short stories. I'll never forget the elation of my first sale, a baseball yarn ("It Shouldn't Happen to a Dodger Fan") to a pulp magazine for $23. I sold a few more stories to low paying pulp and religious magazines. At age twenty-three I met and married Tess. Three months later I was drafted into the Army.

There, for reasons unknown, I was trained to operate data processing (IBM) machines. During my three years in the service I advanced to sergeant and wound up supervising a data processing unit employing scores of military and civilian personnel. I continued writing fiction, sold a few low paying short stories, and collected hundreds of rejection slips. By the time I was discharged at age twenty-six my non-future looked bleak. I of course had no way of appreciating at the time how useful my service and business-related experience would turn out to be to my freelance career later on.

Workplace experience

DELIVERY BOY: merchandise distribution, exposure to customer reactions, role of union during strike, hands-on labor relations experience.

STOCKMAN: customer order fulfillment, inventory keeping experience, departmental interaction (billing, shipping, order, inventory) role of union during organizing activity.

WAREHOUSEMAN: merchandise storage, departmental interaction (production, inventory, shipping, etc.), exposure to grievance procedure, labor relations experience. Exposure to deadly boring grunt work.

UTILITY MAN: manufacturing plant operation, role of union. Packer-shipping and distribution systems, employee grievance procedure, labor relations experience.

MACHINE OPERATOR: manufacturing from production end of the business.

SERVICE EXPERIENCE, U.S. ARMY: data processing background, introduction to technology; experience supervising large groups of people, handling complaints and grievances, human relations; exposure to all kinds of employees—conscientious, average and mediocre, deadbeats who don't give a damn and specialize in work avoidance.

Other than workplace experience

EDUCATIONAL: Understanding and feel for accounting, customer relations, along with profit objective and management responsibilities.

FICTION WRITING: No matter how many books you read, or how many writing courses you take, the learning experience does not exist that can substitute for writing, writing, and more writing. Fiction in particular will help you develop and sharpen your ear for dialogue, useful in all fields of writing endeavor.

So What?

What has all this to do with your concerns as a performing or wannabe solvent freelance? Hopefully, it will open your mind to the value of comparative analysis. While it's true that writers tend to be fiercely individualistic, in my career I have found that again and again there was much to be learned from other writers' experience—and their response to the same problems I ran into and the feelings I felt. You may not react in exactly the same way. But if it provides a launching pad for consideration and judgment, you're that much ahead of the game. At the least it may help you deal with some of the critical questions you will face as a freelance. For example:

What subjects intrigue you the most? In which areas do you perform best and most effectively? What causes inspire you most? What topics are in greatest demand at the moment? Where and how can you most effectively do research? If you view this or that as a problem, how did the other guy solve it?

The experience thus far highlighted covers the period of my life up to my twenty-sixth year following my discharge from the Army. I had always felt the urge to express myself via the written word. But the thought of becoming a freelance never entered my mind. Nor did it occur to me that my disparate scattergun experience would have any significance in this regard. How mistaken I was!

A TIP TO TAKE WITH YOU

With your profession as a freelance in mind, don't sell your experience short—any of it!

Post-military experience (continuing saga of a freelance to be)

Following my discharge from the Army, Tess found a clerical job. I was unemployed with no plans for the future, or inkling of what kind of career I would shoot for. The notion of earning a livelihood as a freelance never entered my mind. But I continued to feel a compulsion to write.

Becoming a father didn't simplify our situation. Nor did the lusty strength of my son Ken's pair of lungs. I took a crack at going into business with my father, if you could call it that. My dad ran a struggling, barely subsistent, one-man "shop" in which he produced ladies' leather handbags and belts. He needed me like the Republican party needs Pat Buchanan, but I felt I could help him make a difference and become financially independent in the process. The arrogance of youth.

In the months that followed, with Ken flourishing, I gained experience as a dad myself, changing diapers, nursing the loudest crybaby in The Bronx through the croup in our tiny one room apartment, and worrying about the mounting bills. Like my father, I did a little of everything in our shop on West 23rd Street in Manhattan: I performed grunt work at the bench, operated sewing, cutting, polishing, and other machines, helped with the books, called on customers and prospects in the field, and learned the business from both the inside and out. Not only learned the business, but got a feel for how it was conducted, and how much deadly routine is involved, all priceless grist for the mill later on. I still didn't know what the future would bring, but I think I felt without actually articulating it, that it would in some way include writing.

I took creative writing courses three evenings a week at Columbia University under the GI bill, and pounded a typewriter in whatever spare time I could find behind the closed door of our tiny bathroom so as not to wake The Shrieking Wonder. The money from the short stories I sold barely covered the cost of the ones that were rejected.

Then suddenly things started looking up. I had designed a line of ladies' snakeskin belts that clicked for a while with orders from stores like Macy's, Bloomingdales, and Sachs. But the bonanza didn't last. It died a quick death when refugees from Argentina began to compete with the stuff we sold at a price below our cost. Times were tough and getting tougher.

After almost two years, to my dad's relief, I cut short my career as an entrepreneur and, after answering hundreds of want ads—bloating my fiction writing experience and submitting samples and short story tear sheets—I landed a job as an apprentice writer for a Broadway publicity agency. There I spent a hectic ten months writing press releases and submitting material to Broadway columnists Walter Winchell, Earl Wilson, Ed Sullivan, and Louis Sobol, et al. I still remember the thrill I felt when I received a phone call from Winchell. "I like your stuff, kid. Keep it coming." In time I did fairly well and had some good "hits" in this madcap game, but found it a one-way trip to the loony bin. The experience cured me of seeking a career as a Broadway publicity writer. Still, I now had writing experience, and damn, if I wasn't becoming a writer. I was also learning how to write humor.

For my next adventure, still a long way from freelance independence or any other kind, I cashed in on my Army service and landed a job as an IBM operator with Atlantic Liquor Co., a wholesaler in The Bronx. I worked there two years until the company went under (through no fault of mine). Now, with a family to support, I was in need of serious money. I answered an ad in *The New York Times* for an IBM Supervisor with wholesale liquor experience, applied for and got the job at Henry Kelly Importing and Distributing Co. on West 14th Street in Manhattan. The company had decided to install an IBM system similar to the one that had worked well at Atlantic, and with which I was thoroughly familiar. But life is never easy. Unknown to me when I was hired, Kelly had previously tried unsuccessfully to install such a setup. This was a last desperate shot at the system, with me as the patsy if it flopped again.

Nerve-wracking as it was, from the standpoint of my ultimate career as a freelance, my personal data bank was fleshing out and diversifying. The job was notable in three respects: 1. I had my first opportunity to manage people in a profit enterprise as opposed to the service which holds little weight in private industry. 2. It fortuitously turned out to be the actual start of my nonfiction writing experience. 3. I engaged in hands-on conflict with no less a giant than IBM.

Heady stuff for a kid in his twenties in his first supervisory job. But it is from such grist-for-the-mill experience that freelance writing careers are fashioned. When I started the job, my boss handed me the specifications prepared by IBM detailing the personnel and equipment needed to get the installation up and running. My eyes popped when I saw the specs. They were wrong in every respect! Wrong equipment, wrong personnel. I knew what was needed from my prior experience, and I knew that this wasn't it.

Swallowing butterflies, I broke the news to my boss. I'll never forget the way he glared at me. IBM had designed this setup. Who the hell was I to question—He didn't say that in so many words. He simply turned heel and walked out. Minutes later the phone rang. IBM's district manager. He set up a luncheon appointment and, accompanied by a sales rep—not the one who had designed the installation—took me to a fine restaurant. Just the three of us.

His first words were, "What's going on here?"

I spelled it out for them. They exchanged doleful looks. I knew I was right, and so did they. The DM said in a more rational voice, "But the system could work, couldn't it?" I reluctantly granted them that. "I suppose it could work, but it would be more costly and less efficient than the configuration I outlined."

They rechecked my specs and agreed. At the DM's suggestion we struck a deal. "We'll go along with your specs as another more efficient way to do the job. But we want you concede to management that our specs can also work but would cost a little more. Otherwise we'll both be out on our butts—you and us." It made sense.

My boss, and his boss, went along with the revised proposal, pleased by the cost reduction. The system was installed and worked smoothly; in fact it became something of a model in the industry. So much so that Gene Murphy, the editor of *Data Processing* magazine, approached me with an invitation to write it up for the magazine. Imagine that! An editor coming to me! I did the article and it was featured as a cover story.

It turned out to be my launching point as a freelance.

Step-by-step up the ladder

I stayed for two years at Kelly, then resigned to take a better paying job as data processing supervisor at Fabergé Perfumes in New Jersey, where we eventually moved. Following the cover story, Gene Murphy accepted virtually every article I sent him—about supervising people, delegating authority, coping with marginal performers, reducing absenteeism, solving problems...you name it. The pay was meager, but those small checks helped out during a difficult period, supplementing my regular income.

Short stories and publicity writing be hanged; all of a sudden I was a business writer with the possibility of earning a living at it in sight. Slowly, gradually, I started branching out with queries to *Office Management, Management Methods, The Office, The American Salesman, Factory*, and other low budget publications. Fees ranging from $50 to $150. I pulled information out of my personal data bank and supervisory experience. I accumulated an abundance of clips to send as samples to prospective editors, a critical part of the freelance's arsenal.

Gathering grist for the mill

My years of experience at Fabergé yielded a treasure chest of information and exposure that served me well in years to come. Here are some of the highlights:

MOTIVATION—I learned as a manager that job performance at all levels from line or staff employee to supervisor to manager to executive to CEO is inextricably linked to the individual motivation that turns employees on and off. I learned too that most people above rank-and-file level fall short when it comes to probing and identifying the needs and desires of the people who work for them. Researching and writing on this subject alone could constitute a freelance writing or consulting career. It has turned out to be one of my most productive and enjoyable specializations.

LABOR RELATIONS—Sadly, in virtually every workplace of twenty-five or more people to which I have been exposed in my lifetime, friction and nastiness erupts on a fairly regular basis. At Fabergé, a young black man in the data processing department was one of the most decent, conscientious, and capable employees in my operation. One day I saw an opportunity to reward him for his effort by transferring him from the day shift to a key job on the 4:00–12:00 shift. He was more than eager to take it. A racist woman would have none of it. "I'm not working with one of them. No way!" It developed into an arbitration case in which my boss and I testified extensively. The woman was fired and the young man promoted. Other cases involving religious and ethnic minorities erupted from time to time. On the plus side, the experience served as groundwork for my *Plant Engineering* column, as well as a subsequent William Morrow book, *Sure Fail—the Art of Mismanagement*, and any number of articles.

BREVITY—My work as a systems analyst, with its procedure writing, report writing, and interoffice communications, helped immeasurably to teach me the value of brevity and elimination of unnecessary words and thoughts. If it doesn't add to the message, delete it. Whatever you write, short, simple, action language reads better and faster than dreary longwinded prose. My boss appreciated this, and so do my readers. Around that time I started a notebook in which I jotted down especially apt action words and expressions I came across in places like *Time* and *Newsweek*, and have been doing it ever since.

MANAGEMENT—My job at Fabergé taught me how to manage, not only my time, which as a writer is critical, but a disparate group of people with differing values, views, and prejudices. I learned that editors in the marketplace are no different from employees in the workplace. I learned, too, the importance of tailoring my own responses and attitudes to the demands of the moment and, in some cases to think twice and once again before making a decision.

STATUS—In writing no less than other professions, personal image adds up to money in the bank. At Fabergé I was my boss's chief adviser. I flooded him with memos suggesting changes and improvements that he could review at his convenience. He appreciated my small publishing triumphs which made him look good as well as myself. He also went along with my self-imposed title changes over the years—from IBM Supervisor, to IBM Manager, to Systems Director. My job was the same, but each title sounded more prestigious than the one it replaced to recipients of my queries and proposals.

TIP OF THE DAY

Whether employed as wage slave or freelance, anything you can do to enhance your personal image is a step in the smart direction.

When an editor reviews your query or proposal, or when a corporate PR exec or communications director sizes you up for an assignment, or when a literary agent ponders whether or not to represent you, what influences the "buying" decision most of all is your image. As an example, my teaching experience at NYU, combined with my status as Systems Director at Fabergé, apparently impressed Wilbur Martin, then editor of *Nation's Business* magazine, enough to trust me with several $500 article assignments, good money at the time. This launched my advance from the puny fees paid by secondary publications to respectable money from the majors.

Peanuts—don't sell them short

One day, while still at Fabergé, I discovered the world of newsletters. There are thousands of them nationwide and worldwide. Name a subject; you'll find a newsletter devoted to it. I don't recall how I first contacted The National Foreman's Institute run by The Bureau of Business Practice. But for several months NFI, which published dozens of newsletters, was a bonanza for myself and my family. Payment for features ranged from $40 or $70 back then. Peanuts? Well, yes and no. But, digging into my supervisory, sales, and labor relations experience, I was able to knock out the short features off the top of my head or with a minimum of research; doing each in an hour or less. In those days it helped to fatten the kitty. I was by now, not a full-time freelance, but a full fledged writer.

I ran across a newsletter called *Better Business by Telephone* published by a Maryland firm. I submitted samples, and for years became a steady contributor. Payment was minimal but steady, and I learned that the more you contribute, the faster your output becomes. For steady, dependable work, it is hard to beat newsletters. A way station on the road to guaranteed solvency. Hack stuff? Perhaps. But the regular income allowed me time for deeper and more serious pursuits. Most important, it allowed time for the causes I espoused, most notably the fair and equal treatment of employees regardless of race, creed, religion, age, gender, sexual, or political preference that was the theme of my book for Morrow and numerous other projects.

A THOUGHT TO TAKE WITH YOU

It has been my experience again and again over the years that often repetitive, low-paying assignments add up to more—sometimes much more—per hour than well-paying gigs requiring extensive research, rewrites, and what-all. A 1,000 word article, for example, that pays $250 and takes a day to complete, is more profitable than a 1,000 word article paying $1,000 that takes five days to complete. If you write on the same subject often enough your productivity will multiply.

One day I had a brainstorm. No goal is more important to corporate executives than increased profits and productivity. Why not a newsletter devoted to that subject? Public relations and promotional expert Dick Conarroe, for whom I had done some work, thought it was a good idea. Between the two of us we spawned *Profit Improvement News*, a "Monthly Roundup of Money-saving Ideas" from corporate America. This was in the pre-desktop publishing era. At $24 a copy, with discount for multiples, over a two-year period we built our subscription list to a little over 1,200. With Tess handling the mailings and administrative end from our basement in Fairlawn, New Jersey, we just barely broke even. When we finally threw in the towel, I was at least able to add newsletter editor and publisher to my list of credentials.

Goodbye Fabergé

Fabergé Perfumes Inc. in Ridgefield, New Jersey, was a good company to work for; my boss, Executive Vice President Phillip Brass, was a great guy to work for. For three years running, having decided to take my freelance plunge full-time, I put in for a preposterous raise at year end, half hoping it would be turned down. Each time to my delight—and disappointment—my boss okayed it. The following year I submitted my resignation. He said I was crazy, that I could have become the company's financial vice president. Great guy that he was, even Phil Brass didn't really know me. I never told him this, but a promotion to financial VP, in my view, would have been a nightmare second to none. Another example of misunderstanding the people you work with and work for, their aspirations, needs, and desires.

By this time, working evenings and weekends, my annual freelance income came to about half of what I would need (minimally) to support my family. I am not by nature a gambler. With Madeleine, another writer-to-be added to the family, I needed the assurance of at least double that income for starters to make ends meet, and for my peace of mind as well. That problem resolved itself in two ways. 1. With more time for prospecting, I picked up a few new corporate clients. 2. I struck a deal with Dick Conarroe to work two days a week as a writer-account executive for The Walden Co., his public relations firm based in New York and Connecticut.

Within a few months my freelance income exceeded my Fabergé salary. Not long after that I discontinued my part-time employment with Dick, went freelance full-time, and added Walden PR with its corporate clients to my growing client list.

Income booster number one

From my personal experience as a freelance, this bears repetition: If you have the training, background and knowhow, and if you can swing it, no category of writing I know pays more, involves less hassles, and yields better treatment than corporate work. My assignments in this field included ghosted books, articles, speeches, brochures, and newsletters for corporate clients, directly, through PR agencies, and via ASJA's Dial-a-Writer service.

Cost reducer number one

I know writers whose annual telephone bills add up to thousands of dollars. A major portion of that expense is ascribed to research, interviews, and discussions with editors. My own phone costs amount to a small fraction of this. These days, with email they have shrunk even smaller. The main source of my savings is that wonderful toll-free 800 number. I have in my files lists of 800 numbers in several categories obtained from the Internet, public library, and elsewhere. In my experience, it's as easy to call a toll free number for information as one where a long distance call adds up to dollars down the drain.

How much should you bill?

A problem confronting every freelance—when dealing with corporate clients in particular—is what to charge for your work, or more accurately, for your time. From one perspective this is a highly personal decision depending on three factors: 1. On an hourly basis, what value do you put on your time? 2. Equally important, how much can you get for your time? 3. Finally, how much can the client actually afford?

I have long used a system that works well for me. Typically, editors and communications executives harbor one major fear in dealing with freelances, that the bill will exceed their authorized budget. From the freelance's perspective it has been my experience that it is often difficult to estimate accurately how long a particular assignment will take. Thus, for me the simple solution is to estimate the project in question on a from-and-to basis, for example, $1,200 to $1,500. This provides the assurance that no matter how long the job takes it cannot cost more than $1,500. In most cases, given this example, my invoice would be $1,400—not greedy, charging the maximum, and well within the client's budget. This arrangement, I've found, tends to keep everyone happy.

The frosting on the cake: "Never a dull moment"

The anti-boredom imperative. This, more than any other reason, is why I am grateful to God—and to Tess who stuck it out with me—that I ultimately chose freelance writing as my career. I think any writer who has experienced the deadly torpor of routine repetitive work will understand just what I'm talking about. Some people can tolerate day after day boredom; no freelance I know could stand it.

One of the great things about a freelance's life is the element of surprise. You never know what unexpected goodies the next day's email, phone call, or trip to the mail box, will bring. For example, during my years in the business:

One day thirty years ago, I got a phone call from Lawrence Stessin, an editor and Hofstra College professor of management, for whom I had done some work. He had received a call from *Plant Engineering* magazine inviting him to write a regular column on labor relations. He was overloaded with work. Would I be interested? Sure. So was launched my column titled, "The Human Side of Engineering," for the most wonderful and generous people in the world, which has been flourishing ever since.

Another time, I received a call from Joe DeParis, data processing manager at Shaeffer Brewery. The class he taught at New York University's Management Institute had experienced overflow enrollment. He knew me from the National Machine Accountants Association, had seen some of my published work, and thought I might be qualified to take on the overflow. Was I interested? "Absolutely." Joe set up an appointment with the Dean. I subwayed down to Washington Square for an interview and, despite being degree-less, my work experience and published articles were enough to qualify me. I was awarded Lecturer status and pay. My image and status, redeemable for big bucks in the writing trade, shot up several notches.

I received a call from one of the world's great editors, Howard Cady, who had edited my William Morrow book, *Sure Fail—the Art of Mismanagement*. He had been asked to recommend an author to give a talk to the New York State Realtors Association at the Concord Hotel in the Catskills. "It's good for a weekend for you and your wife, plus a $500 honorarium. You can pick any one of your books. Are you interested?" I checked with Tess and she jumped four feet into the air. For my spiel I selected *The Complete Book of Walking*, that I had done for Farnsworth/Dutton. The talk was well received, I sold twenty-six copies, and Tess and I had a ball.

Early on, not yet a freelance, a steady source of income was royalties from "rack booklets" distributed by corporations to their employees. Inspirational propaganda on everything from the evils of absenteeism to the values of profits. The articles took a day or two to write and typically yielded about $200. One day an editor called to inform me that my booklet, "Slow Poison" about how and why to control anger had been picked up by GM with its hundreds of thousands of workers and produced royalty income of about $1,500. It kept me happy for days.

Several years ago Wilbur Cross III, a topnotch writer, journalist, and entrepreneur I have been privileged to work for, ran an enterprise called Writers Freelance. I received several great assignments from Will for Fortune 500 clients. One day he called to tell me he was closing down Writers Freelance to sign on as Editorial Director of Continental Oil. "It's perfectly okay with me," he said, "for you to hold on to the accounts you are already serving. You can bill them what you wish and the fee is all yours." Considering that accounts I can recall included IBM, DuPont, and Touche Ross, the Big 8 accounting firm, to name three, it was a bonanza unsurpassed. Will could easily have charged me a commission for jobs done for these accounts, but didn't. That's the kind of guy you meet in the freelance writing profession.

A year or so ago Cheryl Firestone, my *Plant Engineering* editor, flew in from Illinois to interview and photograph me for a feature article, "The Human Side of Ray Dreyfack." Ego nourishment unsurpassed. We all need recognition, writers especially. Thanks to Cheryl's flattering article, I threw away all my old hats. And the status add-on didn't hurt.

Twice I received calls from Norman Guess, my great editor at Dartnell Corporation, that books I had written—*Customers, How To Get Them, How To Serve Them, How To Keep Them*, and *Zero Base Budgeting*—had made the company's direct mail bestseller list. Great for the image-building campaign, greater still for the income-building crusade on the road to Financial Independence as a Freelance Writer.

So it goes for the freelance. Something new every day. An unexpectedly high royalty check, foreign rights picked up and paid for, talk show appearances, celebrity interviews... On and on. Surprises galore.

Oh, sure! Disappointments too. I've had my fair share of them. A favorite editor leaves and his replacement doesn't know me from Abdul. A magazine folds owing me money. A spectacular idea of mine bombs. An already sold article is killed by a dumb new editor. A longtime corporate contact is fired, and me along with her. Royalties on my hoped-for bestseller peter out early on.

Freelancing, like life, has its ups and its downs. But for me, at least, I could contemplate no other career.

The End

ABOUT THE AUTHOR

Ray Dreyfack's freelance career has had its ups and downs, but mostly ups. Once he developed an understanding of how to market his communications skills, he was able to write his own ticket. He didn't jump into full-time freelance writing all at once, though. He understood the necessity of building credentials and relationships on his way to achieving financial independence as a freelance.

Ray's writing spans an amazing range. He's always been willing to try something new, to learn from his fellow writers, and to expand upon previous successes. He has mined his own experiences for story ideas, and he's helped others express the lessons of their work and lives. His magazine writing has resulted in several successful nonfiction books. His love of language and writing has lead him to try his hand at fiction, resulting in one published novel and another unpublished. Writing remains an exciting adventure to him.

The lessons that Ray learned over the course of his very busy career are contained in this book. It is the synthesis of his tremendous experience. No matter the type of freelance writing you may pursue, you'll be well served by Ray Dreyfack's friendly guidance.